To Leslie,

Appreciatively

SIMPLE
HEALTH

DAVID B. BIEBEL, DMIN
HAROLD G. KOENIG, MD

Dave Biebel

SILOAM
A STRANG COMPANY

Most STRANG COMMUNICATIONS/CHARISMA HOUSE/SILOAM products are available at special quantity discounts for bulk purchase for sales promotions, premiums, fund-raising, and educational needs. For details, write Strang Communications/Charisma House/Siloam, 600 Rinehart Road, Lake Mary, Florida 32746, or telephone (407) 333-0600.

SIMPLE HEALTH by David B. Biebel, DMin, and Harold G. Koenig, MD
Published by Siloam
A Strang Company
600 Rinehart Road
Lake Mary, Florida 32746
www.siloam.com

Unless otherwise noted, all Scripture quotations are from the Holy Bible, New International Version. Copyright © 1973, 1978, 1984, International Bible Society. Used by permission.

Scripture quotations marked KJV are from the King James Version of the Bible.

Scripture quotations marked NCV are from The Holy Bible, New Century Version. Copyright © 1987, 1988, 1991 by Word Publishing, Dallas, Texas 75039. Used by permission.

Cover design by Judith McKittrick; cover photo by Getty Images; interior design by Terry Clifton

Library of Congress Cataloging-in-Publication Data
Biebel, David B.
Simple health / David B. Biebel and Harold G. Koenig.
    p. cm.
Includes bibliographical references.
ISBN 1-59185-637-X (pbk.)
1. Health. 2. Mental health. 3. Self-care, Health. I. Koenig, Harold George. II. Title.
RA776.B53 2006
613--dc22

                    2005017514

First Edition
05 06 07 08 09 — 987654321
Printed in the United States of America

Acknowledgments

Dave wishes to thank our two hard-working researchers and encouragers, Bobbie Dill and Sue Foster. Without their help, this book would have been impossible to complete.

Harold wishes to acknowledge his mother, the late Maria Koenig, who trained him early to live a healthy, faith-filled life.

Contents

SIMPLE HEALTH

Wellness Overload

> The two biggest sellers in any bookstore are the cookbooks and the diet books. The cookbooks tell you how to prepare the food and the diet books tell you how not to eat any of it.
>
> —ANDY ROONEY

Diet anxiety. Millions of people have it. Are you one of them? You feel the pressure to look good, feel good—and not succumb to an early death from cancer, diabetes, heart disease, stroke, high blood pressure, or any of the other cataclysmic diseases just waiting to strike those who don't follow the latest diet or spend a month's worth of paychecks on the latest piece of exercise equipment.

Can you relate?

Perhaps you've tried to buy a book on "wellness," thinking it's time to join the rest of the world and finally get healthy, get fit, and get in shape! So there you are, surveying the "health" section of your local bookstore, trying to find a really simple-to-understand and easy-to-practice book on wellness. But you are inundated by a hundred "health" books, seventy "diet" books, fifty diet-recipe books, and another twenty-five exercise-diet-health-recipe books (many of them with matching videos).

SIMPLE HEALTH

On TV, the Internet, and via any of twenty or more health-related magazines, you're barraged with information on similar topics—diets from Atkins to the Zone, supplements from aloe to zinc, alternative therapies from acupressure to yoga, as well as spas and other "wellness centers" that promise the moon for the right price.

Many Americans feel overwhelmed by the constant barrage of information regarding what to eat, what not to eat, how to exercise, and how to avoid contracting disease. Rather than "health information," we are constantly bombarded with "ill-health information" that is focused more on what's going to kill us than on positive ways to look better and feel better. What a comfort it would be to learn that we can improve not only our health but also our well-being in substantial ways—without all of the stress. We can—but we don't necessarily need to join a gym, buy a new weight-lifting machine, or even commit to the newest crazy diet. We can dramatically improve our health with simple, inexpensive, and enjoyable activities—many of which we're doing already! It is possible to live a wonderful and healthy life...simply.

This book is designed to help you relax and not become overly stressed by the news reports that would pressure you into expensive or difficult activities that you *must* do in order to save your health. Our desire is to cut through the barrage of wellness approaches, diet plans, and workout infomercials to embrace the simple patterns of health that will bring the greatest long-term results—a life characterized by wholeness, happiness, and peace. We want to motivate you to move from feeling overloaded by wellness ideas to the realization that you *can* live a simple, happy, and healthy life.

WHAT IS WELLNESS?

Of course, it is assumed that you want to be healthy. We all want to be well. But very few of us have stopped to think through the question, *What is wellness, anyway?* And, *Is wellness really attainable for the average person?* We believe wellness *is* attainable for you, which is why we want to present the material in this book in a way that is understandable, reachable, and even fun for you to pursue. Let's face it, very few of us will ever have the body of Brad Pitt or the beauty of Jennifer Aniston, but it is possible to reach a state of wellness that is just right for you, the wholeness for which you were created. And you do not have to eat tofu for the rest of your life or spend $1,000 on the latest Ab Buster machine to do it.

Most people probably think of wellness in primarily physical terms—in which case good nutrition, hydration, clean air, exercise, and rest are the main issues. Some would add in a mental factor, as in the "mind-body connection," and emphasize that true wellness is only possible when a person is healthy in both body and mind. But we would add that spiritual health is also essential.

In fact, we think that true wellness involves *four* arenas of life: body, mind, spirit, and social relationships. This is because we are all persons with bodies, minds, and spirits who live in the context of relationships—whether we are speaking of one-on-one friendships or our relationship to the entire human race.

Our basis for making this statement is our Judeo-Christian perspective. You will find many of the health-producing practices promoted in this book in the teachings of Moses and the Old Testament prophets and by Jesus and the writers of the New Testament. The Old Testament word for *wellness* is *shalom*, which is often translated "peace" even though its much broader meaning is "whole." The New Testament word is *soteria*, which is often translated "salvation." This word is best understood in the context of healing, health, and wellness. As you conclude this book, you will discover the inner peace and self-acceptance that you seek. Follow the simple principles found in this book, and your health and wellness will improve in amazing ways.

YOU CAN IMPROVE YOUR WELLNESS!

Our goal is to help you improve your overall sense of wellness by reinforcing the health-enhancing habits you already practice and by showing you how to improve in areas that need it—some of which you might not have even considered to be related to wellness.

For example, what does laughter or a good sense of humor have to do with wellness? Or how might recreation or relaxation, anxiety or bitterness play a part? Gratitude, a sense of direction and purpose, or appreciation of beauty—can these really contribute to your overall health in the same way that good nutrition does? Or how do volunteering in your community, generosity, and intimate friendships help you become *and stay* healthy…regardless of how much you weigh?

This is not another diet-exercise-recipe book, but it *is* a "recipe" for wellness, with multiple points to ponder and actions to pursue. It can help you make immediate improvements to your health and wellness, as well as act as a springboard for lifelong changes that will improve your quality of life over time. From exercise to volunteering, you will learn the best and simplest solutions established by science, espoused by experts, and endorsed by Scripture to help lead you to patterns of health in your life. Here are some of the topics we will cover:

- Spiritual health
- A good night's sleep
- Exercise
- Laughter
- Music
- Playtime
- Healthy relationships

Improvement in your overall sense of wellness does not have to be as complicated or as expensive as you might have been led to believe by all those ads and articles. You can improve your life and wellness by placing your focus back on the things that many of us have forgotten—the simple things in life: a good book, a hearty belly laugh, a favorite song, even a long nap on a Sunday afternoon. Practicing wellness may be easier than you ever expected.

OUR CREDIBILITY AND CREDENTIALS

Almost all of what we will say is supported by modern scientific evidence. Where appropriate, we will summarize pertinent studies and cite them so that you can look them up on your own. Altogether we have been involved with more than two dozen books and scores of articles, most of them in the arena of spirituality and health. Harold has been practicing medicine for more than twenty years and is on the faculty at Duke University as professor of psychiatry and associate professor of medicine. He is codirector and founder of the Center for Spirituality, Theology, and Health at Duke University. He is the editor-in-chief of both the *International Journal of Psychiatry in Medicine* and *Science & Theology News.* His research on religion, health, and ethical issues in medicine has been highlighted in *Reader's Digest, Prevention Magazine, McCall's, Time,* the *New York Times, Newsweek,* and many other popular national periodicals. Some of his latest books are *The Healing Power of Faith: Science Explores Medicine's Last Great Frontier, The Healing Connection,* and *New Light on Depression,* which he coauthored with Dave.

Dave holds a doctorate in personal wholeness from Gordon-Conwell Theological Seminary and has been in the ministry since 1974. He has edited Christian medical magazines since 1990—most recently, Focus on the Family's *Physician* magazine (2000–2002) and, since 1992, *Today's Christian Doctor* for the Christian Medical & Dental Associations. He has written extensively in the field of renewal and the journey from brokenness toward wholeness. His most recent involvements include health education.

We offer this brief review of our credentials not to impress anybody, but to let you know that we are in touch with the latest scientific data and other information that you need to know in order to understand how you can have health without the hype, wellness without overload. In terms of the "voices" we'll use, when we say "we," it means we agree on a particular topic. When we disagree, or just wish to express our personal viewpoints, we will make that clear by designating who is speaking.

One thing we *do* agree upon is that we want to help you experience an increased sense of wellness as a result of reading this book and implementing its concepts. But keep in mind, as you read, that there is no such thing as *perfect* wellness. Wellness is dynamic and uniquely defined by each individual. It changes with age, time, and sometimes with circumstances, as in situations when someone may have a terminal illness yet still have a profound sense of wellness that defies human logic. Your sense of wellness will be uniquely your own, and we are here to help you find it.

ESTABLISHING YOUR OWN BASELINE

Because your own wellness can really only be defined for *you*, we would like you to have a baseline idea of how well you are before you get too far into the text. To do so, we have created the "wellness quiz" that appears here and again at the end of the book. A baseline is usually a measurement or score determined at the beginning of a process—for example, a process of medical treatment, which gives the people involved a way of tracking progress as the process continues.

To use this quiz most effectively, before you answer the questions, estimate on a scale of 100 your current overall level of wellness (your wellness quotient). Write that number where asked in the questionnaire. Then answer the questions, compute the results, and see how your total compares with your estimate. After you have read the book and implemented the wellness-enhancing suggestions found in its pages, you will have an opportunity to take the same quiz again and see how your wellness quotient has changed.

We encourage you to read through each chapter at a rate that works best for you in order to absorb and apply the principles to your own life. Read it with a view toward your own wellness, and do not compare yourself with anyone else who may seem to "have it all together." No one, not even those hard bodies and fitness gurus on

TV, will ever experience *perfect* wellness this side of heaven. But that gives us something to look forward to when we get there!

In the meantime, we do believe that there are ways that everyone can improve their wellness quotient in the areas of the body, mind, spirit, and relationships. This is what we want for you as you read through the pages of this book—a new and renewed sense of personal wellness and contentment with who you are and were created to be.

WELLNESS QUIZ

Your wellness quotient estimate: _____

Before you begin the questionnaire, estimate your current wellness quotient (your current overall level of wellness) on a scale of 100, and write it on the line above. Then compare it to the total after you answer the questions.

Answer the questions below before you start reading the book. Enter one number for each question, using the scale of 1-5 below in terms of the degree to which a statement is true of you. If something is *never true,* just leave it blank or enter a zero. After answering all the questions, add your score. The total is your current "wellness quotient." See note below regarding our view of how to understand and use this score.

1   *Not usually true*
2   *Sometimes true*
3   *Maybe/can't decide*
4   *Usually true of me*
5   *Always true*

1. I enjoy a good laugh or good humor. _____

2. I exercise my mind by engaging in creative activity or problem solving. _____

3. I try to manage my stress instead of letting it manage me. _____

SIMPLE HEALTH

4. I get enough sleep and exercise. _____

5. I eat and drink healthy things, do not use tobacco, and use alcohol in moderation or not at all. _____

6. I avoid fad diets. _____

7. I try to keep my living environment as healthy as possible. _____

8. I monitor my health via various means, including regular medical and dental checkups. _____

9. I have at least one friend in whom I can confide. _____

10. I am satisfied with what I have and am thankful for it. _____

11. I find pleasure (or a sense of satisfaction) in my work. _____

12. I value my family relationships and try to protect them through faithfulness and reconciliation. _____

13. I have a sense of purpose, direction, and meaning in life. _____

14. I am a generous and kind person, concerned for those in need (humans and/or animals). _____

15. I work with others to achieve more cooperatively than we might achieve individually. _____

16. I am a happy and optimistic person, savoring life in the present tense. _____

17. My faith in God brings a sense of peace and helps me during times of adversity. _____

18. I engage in religious activities such as prayer, Bible study, devotional reading, or worship. _____

19. I have accepted my own mortality—knowing that I will someday die. _____

20. I have hope, not only in the present tense, but also a
    hope of eternal life when this life is over. _____

Total: My wellness quotient today is: _____

Date: _____ / _____ / _____

This is not a scientific questionnaire, just twenty questions related to wellness. We have observed that people with a score of less than 70 realize that there is room for improvement, and we hope the information in this book will help them make those changes. People with scores of 70–80 have a healthy level of perceived wellness, though there is still room for improvement. People with scores of 80–90 are likely enjoying optimum wellness, while they are also most likely lifelong learners and pursuers of good health. Scores higher than 90 suggest that the individuals involved might benefit by closely reexamining the areas they scored as always true of them, with a view toward whether or not their perception is overly optimistic. Sometimes a trusted friend who knows you well can help with this.

Chapter 1

Laugh Yourself Healthy

Maintaining a Good Sense of Humor

A merry heart doeth good like a medicine.

—PROVERBS 17:22, KJV

A man takes his Rottweiler to the vet. "My dog is cross-eyed. Is there anything you can do for him?" "Well," says the vet, "let's have a look at him." So he picks the dog up and examines his eyes, then checks his teeth. Finally, he says, "I'm going to have to put him down." "What? Because he's cross-eyed?" "No, because he's really heavy."

Are you laughing yet? We certainly hope so, because a good belly laugh is one of the best things you can do for yourself—physically, emotionally, socially, and even spiritually.

One of the simplest ways to improve your quality of life immediately is to laugh. A sense of humor is essential to wellness, and it may even contribute to longevity. As the saying goes, "He who laughs, lasts!" Since the time of Solomon, and surely before, humans have known that "laughter is good medicine." Let's take a look at some of the greatest benefits laughter can bring into our lives.

SIMPLE HEALTH

PHYSICAL BENEFITS

In 1979, Norman Cousins, then editor of the *Saturday Review,* published his book *Anatomy of an Illness as Perceived by the Patient,* which remained on the *New York Times* bestseller list for more than forty weeks. The book describes the author's miraculous recovery from a normally incurable, totally debilitating, and extremely painful disease. "In a sense," he wrote, "I was coming unstuck. I had considerable difficulty in moving my limbs and even in turning over in bed. Nodules appeared on my body, gravel-like substances under the skin, indicating the systemic nature of the disease. At the low point of my illness, my jaws were almost locked."

How did Norman Cousins recover from such a devastating disease? He laughed. And that's no joke! After taking himself off all prescriptions except intravenous vitamin C, he *laughed his way back to health* by watching episodes of *Candid Camera* provided by his friend Allen Funt, viewing old Marx Brothers films, and having his nurse read to him from books of humor during the late night hours. "I made the joyous discovery," he wrote, "that ten minutes of genuine belly laughter had an anesthetic effect and would give me at least two hours of pain-free sleep."[1]

Norman Cousins, who died in 1990, spent the last years of his life as a faculty member of the University of California at Los Angeles School of Medicine, teaching doctors-in-the-making about what Walter B. Cannon had called the "wisdom of the body." This wisdom was also a favorite theme of our late friend and mentor, Dr. Paul Brand, coauthor of *Fearfully and Wonderfully Made* and *In His Image.* Surely, the ability of our bodies to maintain health and to heal themselves when necessary, given proper nutrition and other things they need—including positive emotions arising from laughter—is a gift from God, the author of the body's wisdom, as well as the inventor of laughter.

The sound of roaring laughter is far more contagious than any cough, sniffle, or sneeze. Humor can cause a domino effect of laughter, which brings numerous positive physical effects to the human body. Here are just a few:

Muscle relaxation

The next time you have a good belly laugh, notice how your muscles behave. When you are laughing, the muscles that are not participating in the laughter immediately relax. And as soon as you finish laughing, those muscles that were participating in the laughter relax, too. According to Dr. Paul E. McGhee, research suggests that muscle relaxation almost inevitably results from a good belly laugh. One study that Dr. McGhee cited even showed that people using a biofeedback apparatus were able to relax their muscles more quickly after watching funny cartoons than after looking at beautiful scenery.[2]

Activation of the immune system and reduction of stress

This may seem obvious, but laughter is a great stress reliever, and the research seems to prove it. Dr. Lee Berk and Dr. Stanley Tan demonstrated in a 1996 study that after exposure to humor that caused "large doses of mirthful laughter," the immune system kicked into overdrive for at least twenty-four hours, protecting the person from common colds, germs, or other bacteria that might otherwise have made him sick. In addition, there was a drastic reduction of at least four stress-causing hormones in the bodies of these "laughter participants."[3]

Pain reduction

In one study published by the *Journal of Holistic Nursing*, patients were told one-liners before painful medication was administered and after surgery. The results suggested that those who were exposed to humor perceived less pain when compared with patients who did not receive a "dose" of humor as part of their therapy.[4] According to Dr. Paul McGhee, in another study of thirty-five patients in a rehabilitation hospital, 74 percent agreed with the statement, "Sometimes laughing works as well as a pain pill."[5] These patients had such conditions as traumatic brain injury, spinal cord injury, arthritis, limb amputations, and a range of other neurological or musculoskeletal disorders—so they knew what pain meant, and it meant something when they said that laughter helped. Perhaps Groucho Marx was right when he said, "A clown is like an aspirin, only he works twice as fast."

Cardiorespiratory exercise

Laughter also provides an excellent source of cardiac exercise. The next time you are having a good belly laugh, put your hand over your heart when you finally stop laughing. You will notice that your heart is racing, even after just fifteen to twenty seconds of laughter, and it will remain elevated for three to five minutes. This has caused some physicians to refer to laughter as "internal jogging." You can give your heart a good workout several times a day just by laughing! One physician noted that his patients who said they laugh regularly have lower resting heart rates.[6]

According to Dr. Paul McGhee, recent research indicates that laughter also lowers blood pressure. As your heart beats more rapidly during laughter, it pumps more blood through your system, producing the familiar flushed cheeks. Not surprisingly, blood pressure increases during laughter, with larger increases corresponding to more intense and longer lasting laughs. If this were sustained for hours or days, it might be harmful. But when laughter stops, blood pressure drops back down to its baseline, and many times, below its usual baseline.[7]

Laughter also gives our bodies a good workout. It is great for your diaphragm as well as your abdominal, respiratory, facial, leg, and back muscles. It massages your abdominal organs, tones your intestinal functioning, and strengthens the muscles that hold the abdominal organs in place. Not only does laughter give your midsection a workout, but it can also benefit digestion and absorption functioning, as well. It is estimated that hearty laughter can burn Calories equivalent to several minutes on the rowing machine or an exercise bike.[8]

Authors' Note: For the remainder of this book, whenever we refer to the word Calorie within the context of energy released, we capitalize it. Calorie (or kilocalorie) is used to measure the amount of heat needed to change the temperature of 1 kg of water from 14.5C to 15.5C. It is commonly used in metabolic studies and in reference to human nutrition.

PSYCHOLOGICAL BENEFITS

Movie star Kevin Costner once made this profound statement, "Life's better when it's fun. Boy, that's deep, isn't it?"[9] Kevin Costner was on to something! The benefits of laughter make life "better" all around—not just physically, but psychologically and emotionally as well.

Humor is a powerful emotional medicine that can lower stress, dissolve anger, and unite families in troubled times. Our mood is elevated when we look for humor, even in difficult and frustrating situations. Laughing at the situation and at ourselves helps to reveal that small things are not always the earth-shattering events they seem to be at the time. Looking at a problem from a different perspective can make it seem less formidable and can even help us to find a solution we might not have otherwise seen. Laughter helps us to connect with others and feel less alone.

In psychological terms, laughter helps us to cope not just with work- or stress-related situations, but also with other negative emotional states such as anger, frustration, a sense of helplessness, sadness or depression, embarrassment, shame, or inadequacy. The ability to step back and laugh at yourself or the situation can blow away all of those dark clouds pretty fast.

SOCIOLOGICAL BENEFITS

Dr. Tom Evans once stated, "Laughter is great. Psychologically, sociologically, it's a wonderful tool. It builds trust. It breaks ice. It brings us together. It reaffirms our humanness. Look for opportunities to laugh at yourself or with other people. You have the opportunity to respond with anger or with humor when frustrating situations come your way. Humor is a much better choice for your health!"[10]

Would you rather spend the next three hours with a sourpuss or with someone with a vibrant sense of humor? If you answered, "Sourpuss," then you are in dire need of a good dose of Gary Larson's *Far Side* cartoons. By the way, which one is your favorite? Dave's favorite is the one in which one deer comments on the bull's-eye birthmark on the chest of the other deer, "Bummer of a birthmark, Hal."

In terms of your relationships with other people, nobody is perfect—not you, your spouse, your family members, your friends, your colleagues at work—so the right kind of humor at the right time can help defuse tensions when they arise. If you want to test this, slap on a rubber clown's nose the next time someone tries to pick an argument with you, and just see what happens!

In group settings, humor helps people relax and contribute. Sometimes it even "greases the skids" for open and honest communication in situations where group participants might otherwise feel uncomfortable saying how they really feel. Humor helps others to open up, just as the bartender in the Old West did to a horse that came into the saloon by asking, "Why the long face?"

SPIRITUAL BENEFITS

Unfortunately, many people think that most Christians live in fear that someone, somewhere, is having a good time. But this perception should not be true of believers in Jesus, who frequently laughed and expressed a sense of humor. A healthy, wholesome sense of humor is a reflection of the "joy of the Lord." In fact, the Bible contains a wide variety of humor, and Jesus often expressed a sense of humor, as traced thoroughly by author Leslie Flynn in his book *Serve Him With Mirth.* "I found humor in approximately sixty of the sixty-six books of the Bible," wrote Flynn. He found biblical examples of wit, satire, irony, ridicule, play on words, and other forms of humor employed by prophets, apostles, and some of them even by Jesus Himself.[11] Laughter can sometimes be a sign of our faith; even in the tough times, we can laugh in the face of adversity because we know that God is in control.

In his article "The Winsome Witness," Chuck Swindoll writes, "If you ask me, I think it is often just as sacred to laugh as it is to pray." He gives examples of famous Christian theologians and preachers such as Luther and Spurgeon who loved to laugh. Spurgeon, he says, "infected people with cheer germs. Those who caught the disease found their load lighter and their Christianity brighter."[12]

Without doubt, modern believers do well when they strive to lighten the loads of their fellow human beings through spreading "cheer germs" in the name of Jesus. Good humor and the laughter that goes with it enhance wellness—physically, emotionally, relationally, and spiritually.

So, how can you make laughter a greater part of your life? Here are a few ideas for brightening the world around you through humor and laughter:

- Spend time with people who help you to laugh. In a family setting, try having a "joke night" often.

- Watch or read humor on television or in movies, plays, books, or comic strips.

- Don't sweat the small stuff. Try using a humorous calendar, such as a Far Side calendar by Gary Larson, on your desk to help keep things in perspective.

- When work is getting to you, take a laugh break instead of a coffee break. Take some time out to read jokes on the Internet or listen to a comedy CD in your car.

- Keep a file of good jokes handy in case of a "humor emergency"!

- Visit humorous Web sites on the Internet. Keep the best Web sites bookmarked for later. One such site is http://jokes.christiansunite.com, but there are others. It's a matter of your own taste in humor!

- Share what you find with others, and very soon you'll be forming a comedy club of your own!

So, what's *your* plan? Write it out here.

My Plan

Three things I will do today to make laughter a part of my life:

1. _____

2. _____

3. _____

Three things I will do within the next three months to make laughter a part of my life:

1. _____

2. _____

3. _____

Three things I will do within the next six months to make laughter a part of my life:

1. _____

2. _____

3. _____

Today's date: _____ / _____ / _____

Chapter 2

Exercise Your Mind
Finding a Creative Outlet for Your Unique Skills

> No matter how old you get, if you can keep the desire
> to be creative, you're keeping the child inside you
> alive.
>
> —JOHN CASSAVETES

I magination and creativity are good for you—no matter how old
you are.

If anyone would know this, it would be members of the Senior
Chorale (average age eighty years old) of the Levine School of Music
in Arlington, Virginia, which has performed at the Kennedy Center in
Washington DC. Dr. Gene Cohen, who is studying the health benefits
of creativity as we age, has enlisted members of this group in an ongoing study. "Science has shown that when you challenge older people,
both physically and mentally, they do better," Cohen said. Thus far,
his research suggests that seniors who take on creative challenges are
less depressed, suffer fewer injuries, and go to the doctor less often.[1]
In other words, the challenge of learning, practicing, and performing
has enhanced the quality of life for a group of people whose peers
may be found parked in wheelchairs before TVs in nursing homes. If
involvement in creative activity yields such benefits for octogenarians,

how much greater might be the long-term benefits for you, if you're only sixty, forty, or twenty?

BENEFITS OF CREATIVITY

Expressing your creativity can positively affect your sense of wellness—physically, psychologically, relationally, and even spiritually. And you don't have to paint the ceiling of the Sistine Chapel or write a best-selling novel to gain these benefits! Redecorating your living room or even just keeping a personal journal might produce similar results.

When you were a child, you probably enjoyed doing creative activities, like finger painting, building Lego fortresses, pressing wildflowers, or making things like models, a dollhouse, potholders, or even a tree house. Maybe you sang, played an instrument, kept a diary, wrote poetry, or baked cookies from time to time. I (Dave) recall how when I was about eight years old, I created a "newspaper" of sorts from the cushion sheets of my father's mimeograph machine and then peddled them around the neighborhood. Looking back almost half a century, I can see that young boy then—and now—still putting words on paper, even if these days they are usually published and distributed by someone else.

Nearly twenty years ago, I (Harold) discovered that people who were sick in the hospital depended on their religious faith to help them to cope. This led to my career in the area of religion and health, and it motivated me to learn how to write and do research. Thus, my initial inquisitiveness about how my patients coped with illness led me to conduct research on spirituality, health, and medicine, which takes up most of my time now. These topics are beginning to influence the mainstream medical community as well.

Most people have to lay aside their creative first love, whatever it was, in order to make a living. But in doing so, they have forgotten how to play!

Fortunately, it's never too late to dust off that kazoo, get out the paints, or peck away again on that typewriter (most likely transformed into a computer keyboard by now). Don't be shy; you don't have to perform for an audience or show your creations to anyone. This is not about masterpieces but about peace and mastery.

Benefits of creative expression include:

- Freedom to "color outside the box" (or inside the box, if you make the box yourself)

- Seeing what others don't see and doing something with it or about it

- Increased energy as you pursue something with real passion that seems to well up from deep within

- Delight to the point where you can "work" at it for hours without any sense of time passing

- Confidence that, regardless of what you make or what others might think of it, you really can do whatever it is

- Connection with others who have similar talents or interests

- Communion with the ultimate Creator, who spoke the universe into being

VARIETIES OF CREATIVE EXPRESSION

In reality, there are billions of possibilities here—at least one for each person on the planet. But here are a few examples:

Music and dance

Dance is also universal and as ancient, individual, and cultural as anything can be. Cave dwellers danced to celebrate a successful hunt. In biblical times, people danced to mark their victories. Even today, when major events bring joy to the people, there may be dancing in the streets.

On a personal level, whether your preference is tap dancing, break dancing, ballet, ballroom, disco, river dancing, fitness dancing, or some other type, there are many ways you can express yourself through dance. You can dance to the music all by yourself and have a great time. You could join a dance club, take lessons, or learn to line dance or square dance. The point is the fun of it, plus the physical and social benefits inherent each time you take the floor.

Creative writing—prose and poetry

If you want to write, perhaps the easiest place to start is with what you know best—your own life. Many people keep a diary or daily journal of their experiences, thoughts, and feelings. This process can be both enlightening and healing, partly because as a result of writing something down you suddenly understand its personal importance and meaning more fully. For some people, journaling can be like psychotherapy—with a journal as the therapist. Research published in the *Journal of the American Medical Association* described how journaling about stressful experiences improved the symptoms of patients with asthma or rheumatoid arthritis.[2] Another study, conducted by Kitty Klein, PhD, indicated that writing about stressful events can free up "working memory" (the ability to keep your attention focused in the face of distraction or interference).[3] In other words, it appears that activities that stimulate the mind actually help improve your brain's health.

Poetry is like music in a lot of ways, but without the notes—highly individualistic and subject to personal preference and taste. Some people prefer poetry with rhyme and meter instead of free verse. You may be a person who likes rap. The classification is nowhere near as important as the experience of enjoying or even writing poetry. For some people, poetry seems to force itself to the surface during times of great distress, as in this excerpt from one of Dave's poems after his son's death, which burst from his soul while he was sitting, of all places, in a deer blind during hunting season:

> My boy, the joy had just begun,
> But suddenly your life is done
> And, stunned, I, lonely, wander on
> Without you, an automaton.

I wonder, dare I love again,
Or was our loving all in vain,
A passing pleasure tinged with pain?
Am I to live or just remain?

"Withdraw! Withhold!" my heart replies,
"To love again would be unwise!"
Yet something whispers otherwise,
That only loving satisfies,
Beautifies, or edifies.[4]

When sentiments like these find their way onto a page, it allows you to be able to say, "There; I've said it. That captures it. Maybe now I can move on."

Other kinds of poetry can have wellness benefits, too. Some can be just for fun, like limericks. For example, one unknown poet wrote:

There once was a bear at the zoo
Who always had something to do.
When it bored him, you know,
To go to and fro,
He reversed it and went fro and to.

You could put a poem to music (in the case of rap) or recite poetry to a group of friends, even to your cat or dog. You might try specialized forms of poetry like the Japanese form called haiku. Whatever form of poetry you choose, your creative endeavor will bring health to your emotions, mind, and spirit—and it might enhance your social life. Finally, you might try to illustrate your favorite piece of poetry—mine (Dave's) would be "Stopping by Woods on a Snowy Evening" or "The Road Not Taken," both by Robert Frost.

Painting, sketching, computerized designing

You are never too old or too young to express your artistic talents. Benjamin West began painting at age seven with a brush made of hair clipped from Grimalkin, his cat. Years later, the American painter served as president of the English Royal Academy of Arts. Ann Mary Robertson ("Grandma") Moses took up painting when she was seventy-five, because her arthritis forced her to give up needlework. By her death at age one hundred one, she had painted sixteen hundred paintings, many of them now in art collections worldwide. It seems likely that her painting kept her alert and alive.

When we were growing up, Etch A Sketch and paint by numbers were popular. In today's computer age, children begin manipulating forms on the screen almost before they can talk. Some people use computers to create newsletters, greeting cards, photo albums, or pages they then post on the Internet, instantly accessible to most of the world. All of these endeavors express creativity, exercise the mind, and create a sense of satisfaction. In addition, many of them have positive relational or spiritual benefits.

Photography

The yearning to capture the beauty of creation or the tender expression of a newborn baby or the joy of a bride and groom has led to amazing inventive genius through photography. We may laugh at the old portraits of straitlaced family members on the porch on Sunday afternoon or the comical photos of 1920s' bathing beauties strolling the beaches. Patient photographers often spent hours in the darkroom processing such creations.

But there's also a special emotional and spiritual connection when we come across a photo of our great-grandparents on their way to church in a horse and buggy or the picture of Mom or Dad with their primary Sunday school class or all spiffed up for Easter.

Within the past few years, photography has taken on a whole new dimension that spans the scope of human experience from whimsy to emotion-laden faces to underwater majesty. With the click of our digital camera little bits of our personal and family histories are recorded, then saved for posterity on wafer-thin disks before being archived on computers. We can print out the best shots, in color, with a quality matching modern photographs from slides or negatives.

You can decorate your home with your favorite prints, or you can create an online digital album and send someone you love a "snapshot" of your life in almost real time. The possibilities are limitless and the joy you can share boundless. In this digital age, anyone can be creative with just the touch of a button and the click of a mouse.

SIMPLE WAYS TO DEVELOP YOUR CREATIVITY

Start small

Your project doesn't have to be perfect on your first attempt! It's OK to start small. But no matter what you create, you have the right to be proud of yourself.

Follow your heart

Others may offer advice, but many times their values and yours will not agree in relation to anything you might create. As the "Athletes in Action" say, "When I perform, it is for an audience of one." Perhaps you interpret this statement to mean that the only important audience is yourself. But in their case, they're thinking of the Lord.

Become a lifelong learner

Don't be afraid to expand your interests. Many people never stray far from what they already know. But real satisfaction and unexpected joy can come from venturing into something totally new. This new endeavor can be something as simple as trying to learn a new language or learning the meaning of one new word per day in your own language. Numerous Web sites are available to help with this, including www.webster.com. Learning activities like these help to exercise your brain and provide some protection against deterioration—in other words, learning exercises help your brain stay healthy just as physical exercise helps your body.[5]

Constantly ask "why" or "what if" questions

Creative people are not usually members of the "status quo" society. They are usually questioners, trying to create what isn't or to improve what is. The latter is the driving force of most inventions.

One of my (Dave's) friends, musician Matt McPherson, wondered why the hole in acoustic guitars had to be right under the strings. He wondered whether, if the hole were moved and reconfigured, the guitar might sound better. Bottom line—he invented a new acoustic guitar, far superior in sound to anything before it. I'll never forget that day a few years ago in Matt's office when he played his prototype for me. McPherson guitars are rapidly gaining popularity among professionals and amateurs.

Find pleasure and deep satisfaction in the creative process

In making anything you are imitating God. When you create, you express perhaps the most significant part of His image that you bear, the ability to create...starting with just an idea. In a sense, this makes you a co-creator with Him, even if only on a small scale. Surely, nothing could be more wellness enhancing than that!

OTHER SUGGESTIONS FOR EXERCISING YOUR MIND

- Participate in amateur theater and talent shows. Theater is a great forum for creative expression and a great place to make new friends. You can participate in many ways beyond acting, dancing, or singing—for example, storytelling, painting or staging, script writing, or costuming.

- Tap your originality—originality involves starting from scratch or starting from something that exists and improving it.

- Engage in problem solving, including doing crossword puzzles or playing other games, such as chess.[6]

- Express yourself—uniquely, without trying to emulate or copy somebody else and without worrying about what others may think of your creative expression.

- Expose yourself to new things that stimulate your mind and imagination—listen to beautiful music, visit museums, travel, study the lives of inspirational people, enhance your productivity, and follow your dreams.

• Expand your relational horizons to include creative and/ or eccentric people who are not afraid to take risks.

• Apply the following skills to the creative endeavors you choose to pursue: dedication, hard work, actively seeking new challenges or horizons, boldness, and willingness to follow your creativity wherever it may lead you.

Just adding a little creativity and imagination to your life can improve your wellness and help you to live a happier, healthier life. So...what's your plan to exercise your mind through creativity? Write it out here:

My Plan

Three things I will do today to exercise my mind:

1. _____

2. _____

3. _____

Three things I will try to do within the next three months to exercise my mind:

1. _____

2. _____

3. _____

SIMPLE HEALTH

Three things I will try to do within the next six months to exercise my mind:

1. _____

2. _____

3. _____

Today's date: _____ / _____ / _____

Chapter 3

Manage Your Stress
Learning to Let Yourself Relax

Come with me by yourselves to a quiet place and get
some rest.

—MARK 6:31

Perhaps this is a day in the life of someone you know:

6:00 a.m.: Wakes up, works out to a dance video, showers,
dresses, gulps down cup of coffee #1

7:00 a.m.: Fixes breakfast for husband and kids, swigs down
cup of coffee #2, starts the laundry, feeds hubby and
sends him off to work, gets kids up and dressed, forces
them to eat their breakfast, straightens up the house,
gathers things for the church rummage sale

8:00 a.m.: Carpools the kids to school

9:00 a.m.: Starts cup of coffee #3, starts laundry, answers
phone (mother-in-law complaining), neighbor shows up
for coffee and needs to talk

9:30 a.m.: Dog throws up

9:35 a.m.: Neighbor leaves

10:00 a.m.: Takes dog to vet; pays $296 for exam, X-rays, and treatment; first two credit cards are declined

11:00 a.m.: Restarts laundry, cleans kitchen, garbage disposal clogs up, calls husband to bring home parts

12:00 p.m.: Grabs chips and dip (lunch) while laundry dries, answers phone and fields complaints about rummage sale chairperson, considers another cup of coffee—or stronger, settles on green tea

1:00 p.m.: Drops rummage sale items off at church, listens to more complaints

2:00 p.m.: Grocery shops for nice dinner—since husband will leave on a five-day business trip in the morning, decides to get hair done to look nice for him that evening

3:00 p.m.: Picks up kids, takes to soccer practice, rain ruins hair

4:30 p.m.: Makes quick stop at Wal-Mart on the way home for cleaning supplies, kids whine for candy in the checkout line and cause a scene in public

5:00 p.m.: Starts gourmet seafood dinner, grilled portobello mushrooms with salmon and spinach stuffing, while refereeing kids' argument about video game

6:00 p.m.: Serves dinner, which husband loves but kids hate; kids feed their dinner to the dog when mom is not looking

7:00 p.m.: Cleans up kitchen while helping husband with garbage-disposal repairs, oversees kids' homework, fantasizes about putting *them* in the disposal, makes phone calls regarding the church rummage sale—stifling the desire to tell people off

8:00 p.m.: Oversees kids' way-too-long process of getting ready for bed, reads them a story, says prayers

9:00 p.m.: Irons and folds laundry, helps husband pack for business trip—"biting tongue" when he mentions that some of his best clothes don't fit anymore since he's gained twenty pounds this year

9:30 p.m.: Sits down in a comfortable chair for the first time all day, dog immediately throws up again—salmon and mushrooms this time, administers sedative to dog, husband tries to snuggle, considers giving husband a sedative also, but instead...

10:00 p.m.: Watches a short movie with him in bed, and then...

11:30 p.m.: Sets clock for 5:00 a.m. to get hubby off to the airport, falls asleep while humming, "Momma said there'd be days like this..."

STRESS, DISTRESS, AND YOUR HEALTH

Perhaps you can identify with a day like this, or perhaps not, but modern life is full of stress, even if you're not a "soccer mom." Everyone has stress. Some of us have a little. Some of us have a lot. Much of our stress comes from sources beyond our control, but sometimes stress comes from areas of life that we can learn to control. Wouldn't you love to live a calmer, more stress-free life? Do you even think that is possible? It is—and you don't have to spend thousands of dollars in a therapist's office to make it happen for you!

Acute stress

Some stress is *acute*, which means that it happens suddenly and then goes away within a short period of time. For example, let's say you're out for a casual walk and encounter a big, unfriendly dog. Here's the sequence of events:

1. In response to seeing the dog, and expecting a hostile encounter, you reach for the pepper spray, only to remember you left it home.

2. The dog growls, and a certain part of your brain (called the hypothalamic-pituitary-adrenal [HPA] system) kicks into gear.

3. The HPA system triggers and releases hormones, including cortisol, which is like your body's "General," directing the troops you need in order to avoid or deal with a dog bite: heart, lungs, circulation, metabolism, immune system, skin.

4. The HPA system releases chemical messengers to the brain, including adrenaline, which kicks in your "fight-or-flight" mechanism, since you're either going to have to fight the dog or run like mad.

5. As the dog approaches, your heart rate and blood pressure increase.

6. Blood flow increases dramatically—300 percent or more.

7. Your spleen discharges red and white blood cells.

8. Your immune system prepares for possible attack.

9. Your mouth goes dry, and your throat feels tight.

10. Your skin feels cool, damp, and sweaty, and your scalp tightens so your hair stands up.

11. Your digestion shuts down.

12. You enter "fight-or-flight" mode, looking for a rock or stick. Then, when the dog seems to lose interest, you get out of there—as fast as you can.

13. After a few minutes in a safe place, all your systems return to normal.

Obviously, your body's response to acute stress is not necessarily a bad thing. In caveman times, when the "dog" was a saber-tooth tiger instead, for example, your response might have saved your life. Today it helped you avoid a dog bite and an expensive visit to the emergency room.

Chronic stress

Chronic stress—stress that lasts a long time—is a different matter. Chronic stress comes from things like long-term high-pressure or unpleasant work situations, long-term relational problems, illness, loneliness, financial worries, or other things that weigh you down. It produces a physical response similar to what happened when you met that dog, but as long as the situation causing the stress is "in your face" or on your mind, your whole system remains in the "fight-or-flight" mode.

Chronic stress can make you sick or kill you, unless you manage it well. Here's a list of symptoms related to chronic stress—listed alphabetically. Although many people experience one or more of these for a short duration from time to time, if you experience several of these on a regular basis, your stress most likely needs better management, including some advice and treatment from your personal physician:

- Abdominal pain
- Always feeling uptight or on edge; racing thoughts
- Always on the go, and often late to the next scheduled appointment
- Anger when you have to wait
- Diarrhea
- Difficulty concentrating, even on spiritual things such as devotional reading

- Difficulty finding the humor in something even when others do
- Dizziness, shakiness, or muscle twitching
- Eating problems: overeating with weight gain or under-eating with weight loss
- Fatigue or weakness, even though you haven't exerted yourself
- Feeling overwhelmed, but still unable to say no to more
- Fixation on negative things, such as guilt or remorse
- Flare-ups in ulcers or bowel diseases
- Headaches
- Heart palpitations
- Hair loss
- Irregular breathing patterns
- Irritability, sometimes with angry outbursts that seem beyond control
- Lingering sadness
- Menstrual problems
- Mood swings
- Muscular and joint pain
- Nausea or vomiting
- Nervous activities (foot tapping, nail biting, teeth grinding)
- Night sweats
- Pelvic pain
- Problems remembering
- Sensation of lump in the throat
- Spasms of the esophagus, bladder, or bowel
- Stuffing your feelings
- Substance abuse (caffeine, nicotine, alcohol)
- Tightness or pain in the chest area
- Trouble sleeping
- Trying to do everything "just right"
- Upper respiratory problems

- Weighed down by financial concerns
- Worried what others think of you
- Worried that you may become seriously ill

Symptoms like these, when they last a long time, can contribute to the development or worsening of specific illnesses, including the following:

- Asthma
- Cardiovascular disease
- Chronic fatigue syndrome
- Circulation problems in hands and feet
- Clinical depression
- Fibromyalgia (widespread chronic pain)
- Frequent colds
- Gastroesophageal reflux disease (GERD)
- Hypertension (high blood pressure)
- Irritable bowel syndrome
- Migraine headaches
- Stomach ulcers
- Stroke
- Temporomandibular joint syndrome (TMJ)[1]

DETERMINING YOUR LEVEL OF CHRONIC STRESS

Before you try to manage your stress level, you may need to get a more realistic picture of how much stress you actually have. So here is another quiz, using a 0–2 scoring scale this time and fifty questions. It is not a substitute for diagnosis or treatment of any disorder, just a tool to help you gauge your own "stress level."

STRESS QUIZ

0   *Does not describe me*
1   *Sometimes describes me*
2   *Describes me/usually true of me*

SIMPLE HEALTH

Score for each question:

1. I am always on the go, with a long "to do" list. _____

2. I have headaches quite often, or sometimes I feel as if my head is "in a vise." _____

3. I get upset when I have to wait, for example, in traffic, in a store, or at a doctor's office. _____

4. I keep my true feelings to myself most of the time until I lose control and blow up. _____

5. I have trouble falling asleep or staying asleep once I do. _____

6. I know I need to get more exercise, but I can't seem to get to it. _____

7. When I'm under pressure, I often skip breakfast and then snack throughout the day. _____

8. I smoke, drink, or use tranquilizers. _____

9. I do most things myself because I can't trust others to do them right. _____

10. I have pains in my muscles or joints that are not related to injuries or illness that I know of. _____

11. I have trouble concentrating on one thing at a time. _____

12. I have problems with my stomach or digestive tract. _____

13. Even when others are laughing about something, I find it hard to share the levity. _____

14. I sometimes have trouble breathing or tightness or pain in my chest when I am under pressure. _____

15. Sometimes my heart seems to be racing or skipping beats. _____

16. I think that recreation is basically selfish or a
waste of time. _____

17. At the end of the day, I rarely feel that I have done
enough. _____

18. I take things seriously most of the time. _____

19. I feel that it is in my best interest to hide some of my activities from those who are close to me. _____

20. I consume more than three caffeine-rich drinks per day. _____

21. I have a disability or chronic illness that limits many of my
choices and opportunities. _____

22. I can't seem to find time for prayer or devotional
reading, though I know they would be good for me. _____

23. I don't like to participate in social activities such as
parties, church suppers, dancing, or reunions. _____

24. I have developed nervous habits such as foot tapping, nail biting, or grinding or clenching my teeth. _____

25. Sometimes my muscles twitch or I feel shaky or
dizzy for no reason. _____

26. It is difficult for me to just stop, rest, or enjoy a
little solitude. _____

28. At work I feel under constant pressure, no matter
how well I perform or how much I accomplish. _____

29. I have some relational problems pressing me down—
marriage, children, extended family, friends, and so on. _____

30. Sometimes I feel trapped by (or stuck in) my life in
general and helpless to do anything about it. _____

31. I never play games just for the fun of it—such as
solitaire, charades, or board games with family/friends. ____

32. My marriage status recently changed—married or lost my spouse to death, divorce, or separation. _____

33. I recently experienced the death of a family member (not my spouse) or close friend. _____

34. I (or my spouse) recently started a new job. _____

35. I recently moved. _____

36. I don't have a pet because I don't have time or energy for one. _____

37. I was recently diagnosed with a serious illness or condition._____

38. I recently left one church and started attending another._____

39. I seem more prone to viral infections, such as colds, than others. _____

40. No matter how much I accomplish, I usually feel I could have done better. _____

41. I recently experienced a significant financial reversal. _____

42. I do not have time for a hobby. _____

43. My family size recently changed—added someone through birth/adoption; someone died or moved out. _____

44. I am anxious about an upcoming holiday, anniversary, birthday, or special event. _____

45. I am trying to get ready for an upcoming vacation. _____

46. I am concerned that my/our debt is too large. _____

47. I attend a church that often passes judgment on individuals or groups. _____

48. I rarely attend or watch sporting events. _____

49. I rarely go out for dinner or a movie because they are a waste of time and money. _____

50. I avoid being around people whose ideas, values, or actions I don't approve of. _____

Total: My stress level today is: _____

I would prefer it to be about: _____

Note: Although this is not a scientific instrument, it is a composite of a variety of self-scored stress questionnaires available online or in books and articles. This quiz is for your benefit, to give you a numeric value for your own perceived stress. We feel that scores 0–25 mean you do not have much stress or that you are managing your stress very well. Scores of 26–50 may indicate that you are managing your stress reasonably well, though there is room for improvement. Scores of 51–75 may indicate that your stress is significantly affecting your overall wellness and that you could benefit from learning and using some stress-reduction techniques. Scores over 75 suggest that changes are urgently needed and that obtaining professional assistance would be wise.

MANAGING YOUR STRESS

Now that you've identified certain things that increase your stress, along with symptoms you sometimes experience as a result, it's time to decide what should be changed in order for your health to improve. Once you have created this list (you may need to review the quiz you just took), try following one or more of the following simple solutions to stress management.

1. Take control.

From finances to your job, deadlines to relationships, there is almost always something that you can do to change the situation or to change its impact on you—physically, emotionally, relationally, or spiritually.

Our friend and colleague Dr. Richard Swenson has written two books related to this subject, which we highly recommend: *Margin* (1992) and *The Overload Syndrome* (1998). In the latter book, he describes one fateful Tuesday night in 1982 when he and his wife, Linda, changed the direction of their life. Sitting before the fireplace on the floor of their living room, they took out a pad of paper and wrote down everything they could about their lives at that moment— including attitudes, activities, beliefs, influences, hopes, dreams, and possessions. Then they tore up the paper and burned it. They then "gave the pencil to God," asking Him to redesign their lives according to what was fully and spiritually authentic. "It was an exciting evening," Dick wrote. "An exhilarating sense of freedom swept over us. As we wrestled control of our lives away from the world, we felt the elephant slipping off our backs....Our redesigned life was simpler. That decision reduced our income significantly, but the freedom, the time, the rest, and the balance have all been well worth it. We have never looked back."[2]

While it may not seem practical to approach your own life, including its stressors, in exactly this same way, you might try some type of creative variation. The important point is that you remain open to change and willing to do what it takes in order to achieve your true goals. You are not a victim under the influence of forces beyond your control. But change can be scary, because it takes you toward the unknown or possibly the unknowable. In the case of Dr. and Mrs. Swenson, in whose home I (Dave) have stayed several times, this total rewrite of their life's direction led Dr. Swenson away from medicine and into writing. But it has taken them far and wide in an attempt to alert the government, society, the church, and individuals like you and us to the dangers and stressors of modern life and what can be done about them.

2. Develop a hobby.

Hobbies come in as many forms as there are hobbyists, but here are a few potentially stress-reducing ones:

Collecting. Novelist Ayn Rand described the emotional and sociological benefits of collecting stamps: "In stamp collecting, one experiences the rare pleasure of independent action without irrelevant burdens or impositions. Nobody can interfere with one's collection, nobody need be considered or questioned or worried about. The choices, the work, the responsibility...and the enjoyment...are one's own. So is the great sense of freedom and privacy.

"For this very reason, when one deals with people as a stamp collector, it is on a cheerful, benevolent basis. People cannot interfere, but they can be very helpful and generous. There is a sense of 'brotherhood' among stamp collectors, of a kind which is very unusual today; the brotherhood of holding the same values."[3]

Some people collect stamps, shells, dolls, antique cars, or baseball cards. In one family we know, the husband collects rocks, the wife collects old books, the older son and daughter collect, press, and categorize wildflowers, and the youngest son collects bugs.

Needlework. Sewing and handwork in the form of needlepoint, cross-stitch, knitting, quilting, or spinning bring hours of relaxed pleasure to many. The medium, colors, and form you choose are only limited by availability of material and your time and energy as you create original things of beauty to use or give to special people. The stress-reduction value is in the process, not in what you do with the result.

Yet handiwork also tells a story about its creator, and distinctive pieces often become family heirlooms. What might begin as necessity (clothes for the new baby or blankets for the approaching winter) can quickly become expressions of love and beauty. These forms of art are often passed down from one generation to the next—creating a special link between family members. Certain cultures produce exquisite handiwork—for example, the colorful beadwork of the Native Americans or the breathtaking quilts designed by the Amish. Working on creative handiwork projects in a group setting can be the source of great personal satisfaction and vibrant friendships.

Woodworking. In his article "Get Into a Hobby: It's Good for You!" Bill Malone wrote, "Hobbies are great distractions from the worries and troubles that plague daily living. I myself have an interest in woodworking, and I recently took a woodturning course and found that when I am turning a project I am not thinking about work, my failing eyesight, or the house chores. I find myself lost in the creative endeavor. Several hours pass without looking at the clock. My mind is quiet and still and my attention is on creating a masterpiece out of a hunk of firewood. Even if a masterpiece is not discovered, what I have acquired is time spent in creating and making a lot of woodchips. I now know how Michelangelo felt as he chipped away the excess marble to find David inside...."[4]

3. Seek and enjoy solitude.

Modern life seems to include constant interruption and background noise of some kind—traffic, TV, phone calls, radio chatter and advertising, computer games, videos—most of the time. So solitude may seem strange at first. But if you really want to reduce your stress, getting out into God's creation is a good place to start. Where you go is a matter of personal preference—to the mountains, a park, a botanical garden, to a lake, or the seashore. All these can have a calming effect, enhancing your enjoyment of life. Henry David Thoreau wrote: "I went to the woods because I wished to live deliberately, to front only the essential facts of life, and see if I could not learn what it had to teach, and not, when I came to die, discover that I had not lived."[5]

An alternative to this might be to turn on the phone answering machine—remember that the phone is there for your convenience, not the convenience of others. Find a quiet place in your home where you will not be disturbed for at least thirty minutes, lie down in a comfortable spot, and listen to nature sounds or relaxing sounds via your stereo system with headphones. You can purchase music CDs on these themes or download the music via the Internet by doing a search for "nature sounds" or "relaxing nature sounds." The most important matter here is not what you choose, but that on a regular basis, once or twice a day, you take a break in which you can relax and unwind.

4. Look for humor in the situation.

Stress often comes from how we interpret and judge the world we live in. But humor can be used to think about a situation in a different way. Loretta LaRoche says, "Take the sting out of stress by accepting what you can't change, changing what you can, and laughing at the rest."[6]

Laughter is truly the best medicine for some ailments. It is impossible to laugh and cry at the same time. If you learn to laugh at others and laugh at yourself, you will learn to take life less seriously. In fact, the word *silly* comes from the ancient Latin word *selig*, which means "to be blessed."[7] In your life today, which are you: stressed or blessed?

5. Pray and connect yourself to the Eternal—and stay connected.

Prayer can be an effective antidote for stress. In the past people have used prayer books and formulas for this—prayers that were read aloud in the morning, midday, afternoon, evening—mostly practiced by monks and others with little else on their "to do" list. To have little else on your mind but the worship and adoration of God—this will work wonders for your body as well as your soul. But in today's world, such monastic practices are extremely hard to follow.

Even though Eastern religious practices seem to dominate the media in terms of meditation, Christian meditation begins when you quiet your soul before your Creator and think about Him. And prayer is far more than repeating some words composed by someone else, though this may help get you into the proper frame of mind. The apostle Paul said that we should "pray continually" (1 Thess. 5:17), so he must have been describing an inner reality. When you invite God's company on your day's journey, you can have ceaseless communion and perpetual dialogue with your Creator—without the prayer book.

Prayer isn't something you do as a means to an end. It is an attitude, part of who you are, a practical way to know God and be known by Him...in the present, where He constantly dwells. In other words, when you are spiritually connected to Him life can be one long prayer, like staying on the phone with someone whose company you enjoy.

ADDITIONAL SUGGESTIONS FOR MANAGING STRESS

As the ancient proverb says, "The bow that is always bent will break." If your stress levels are high, based on the symptoms, diseases, or the quiz in this chapter, then you probably need to make some different choices—or your stress may make the choices for you. If you have found that your stress level is unacceptably high, begin to try to reduce it through the means just listed or by the following:

- Take a walk or exercise every day. According to C. Krucoff in his article "Pump Up Your Spirit," one study has shown that repetitive exercises, such as walking, cycling, or swimming laps, can have an extremely calming effect, in much the same way as a baby who is being rocked to sleep.[8]

- Learn and employ methods of physical relaxation.

- Get the perfectionism monkey off your back—you don't have to please your parents any more or even meet the unrealistic expectations of yourself or others.

- Be sure you get enough sleep—seven to eight hours per night is normal.

- Enlist the help of a support group—friends who understand and love you—and stay close to them.

- Build your reserves, whether physical, financial, emotional, or spiritual. Then when stress hits, exhaustion or depletion is less likely. Good nutrition, including a diet rich in whole foods—fruits, vegetables, grains, dairy, and protein—will help you establish and maintain optimum physical health. Just don't binge on chocolate, as many of us do under stress!

- Play—whenever you can, for as long as you can; even in bits and pieces, play reduces stress.[9]

- Pat your pet—but if your only pet is a goldfish and it purrs, perhaps you're more stressed than you thought. Joke.

So what's your plan? Write it here.

My Plan

Three things I will do today to reduce and manage my stress:

1. _____

2. _____

3. _____

Three things I will try to do within the next three months to reduce or manage my stress:

1. _____

2. _____

3. _____

SIMPLE HEALTH

Three things I will try to do within the next six months to reduce or manage my stress:

1. _____

2. _____

3. _____

Today's date: _____ / _____ / _____

Chapter 4

Get Enough Exercise and Rest
Listening to Your Body and Giving It What It Needs

> I have never taken any exercise except sleeping and
> resting.
>
> —MARK TWAIN

Perhaps you heard about the guy who joined a health club. A year later, he stopped by to renew his $500 membership, but he was even more flabby and out-of-shape. When he mentioned this to the receptionist, she reviewed the record, and said, "Perhaps it would help if you would stop in once in awhile."

Everybody knows that regular exercise is a key to health. That's why billions of dollars are spent each year on health club memberships, exercise equipment, and related products. But instead of being used to work up a sweat, here are a few tongue-in-cheek typical uses for some of the more common items of equipment in question:

Dumbbells and *barbells* can make good meat tenderizers. Using them this way adds iron to your diet and gives your shoulders and arms a workout. Using barbells as tandem meat tenderizers is possible but a bit trickier, as each steak must be precisely placed on the floor before the barbell is dropped on it. These devices can also be used to roll cookie dough, but it's messy and the cookies usually emerge from the oven with wavy tops.

47

Ab rollers can be used to knead dough for bread or pizza if you put the dough below the headrest and rock rapidly back and forth on it. Or if your kids use flying saucers for sledding, you can enclose them in one of these in case they roll over on the way down the hill.

Other ab and bun devices that you sit and rock in can often be used to help you impersonate starship captains or racecar drivers. Those with two handles are useful for hanging large flowerpots or arrangements, or as a bouncing swing for the baby when hung close enough to the floor.

Thigh workout devices that you squeeze together between your legs make great door closers, as long as you remember to jump out of the way in time. They can also be adapted for delivering stern warnings to bears or other troublesome wild animals.

Stair steppers and other similar devices provide nice alternative decor in your rec room. For example, family photos can be placed on the steps, with their elevations varied from time to time.

Treadmills can be useful when the dog needs a good workout, and you don't have time to go for a drag. With a bone or piece of meat properly positioned just out of the dog's reach, you can watch a good movie from your rocker while the dog tries to get to the bone.

Exercise bikes, if they have spokes, can be used as vertical food processors. An alternate use, assuming the wheel's surface is rough enough, is to sharpen tools, knives, or skate blades. If yours has a belt attached, you may be able to adapt the belt to hold the tools in place, freeing your hands for eating chips and salsa.

"Bullworker" universal gyms, designed for upper body workouts, can be fun for your kids to use when impersonating a kangaroo at a costume party. Alternate uses include nailing things to the ceiling or other hard-to-reach places.[1]

Having acknowledged what sometimes happens to those expensive pieces of equipment we buy in hopes of getting more exercise, let's think about exercise realities and the fact that you can get fit and stay fit without spending a lot of money.

EXERCISE WILL IMPROVE YOUR LIFE

Scientific studies have shown repeatedly that all of the following are true. References to relevant articles are listed in the notes in case you want to read more on any particular subject.[2]

- Regular physical activity reduces your risk of *coronary heart disease, stroke,* and *colon cancer.*

- Regular physical activity reduces the risk of developing *type 2 diabetes* or *high blood pressure.* It also helps reduce blood pressure in people who already have high blood pressure.

- Regular physical activity can reduce *stress* and feelings of *depression* and *anxiety.*

- Regular physical activity can help relieve or prevent back pain.

- Regular physical activity promotes bone formation and may help prevent osteoporosis or other forms of bone loss associated with aging.[3]

There are basically three types of exercise: stretching, aerobic exercise (that works your heart and lungs), and weightlifting. Stretching is important for flexibility and to warm up if you're about to engage in something more strenuous. Although it would seem that there's nothing very formal about stretching, some experts have identified at least seven different types of stretching as well as several classifications of flexibility.[4] For most people, however, some of the best stretching activities are yoga-type exercises. These are promoted regularly in health magazines and also described on the Internet in various places. (If you type in "yoga stretching," you'll get as many as twelve thousand matching sites.) Just keep in mind that it's not about turning yourself into the shape of a pretzel, but about keeping your muscles in tone. And it's not about being a Hindu, either. You can easily implement the exercises without the philosophy.

Cardiovascular exercise is anything that forces your heart and lungs to work a little harder than they do when you are at rest. This would include jogging or running, but it also includes walking—an underrated way to get the exercise you need. According to *Walking: The Natural Way to Fun and Fitness*, produced by the American Heart Association, studies have demonstrated that walking has many benefits,[5] including mental functioning even in the elderly.[6]

When you think of weightlifting, images of bodybuilders may come to mind. But lifting weight does not have to be "formal" as in lifting barbells or dumbbells, nor does it have to involve lifting heavy weights in order to be effective for keeping muscle tone, since repetition using lighter weights will achieve the same thing. Weightlifting is particularly important as we age to retain muscle strength and tone. When people lift weights to bulk up, rather than to increase muscle strength and tone through repetition of lighter weights, as soon as they stop lifting weights, the muscle quickly turns to fat and flab. So, if you want to lose weight and trim up, using heavy weights is definitely the wrong way to go over the long run.

FIT *AND* FUN

The Centers for Disease Control and Prevention (CDC) recommends some physical activity on most days of the week, preferably daily—five days or more weekly if moderate-intensity activities are chosen (walking or gardening); three or more days weekly if vigorous-intensity activities are chosen (running, swimming, or cycling). An effective plan, depending on your age and condition, might be to alternate your types of exercise.

"Moderate activity," according to the CDC, is exercise that uses approximately 150 Calories of energy per day, or a thousand Calories per week.[7] Calories measure the energy released when your body breaks down food. The more Calories a food has, the more energy it can provide to your body. When you eat more Calories than you need, your body stores the extra Calories as fat. How this happens will depend on your weight, the type of exercise involved, and how long you do it.

Here is an estimate of how many Calories are used by people in four different weight groups during each fifteen-minute period of nonstop involvement in the activities listed:

NUMBER OF CALORIES BURNED IN FIFTEEN MINUTES OF ACTIVITY[8]				
Activity	130 pounds	150 pounds	170 pounds	190 pounds
Sitting (reading or watching television)	20	23	26	29
Playing with kids: vigorous effort	98	113	128	143
Cleaning house: general	59	68	77	86
Child care: bathing, feeding, etc.	59	68	77	86
Gardening: weeding	88	101	115	128
Mowing lawn: push, hand	117	135	153	171
Walk: 3.5 mph (17 min/mi)	74	86	97	108
Rollerblade/In-Line skating	244	281	319	356
Golf: walking and pulling clubs	84	97	110	123
Skiing: cross-country, light effort, 2.5 mph	137	158	179	200
Swimming: leisurely, no laps	117	135	153	171
Swimming: crawl, moderate, 50 yds/min	156	180	204	228
Bicycling: 12-14 mph, leisure	156	180	204	228

Activity	130 pounds	150 pounds	170 pounds	190 pounds
Stretching: mild, yoga	49	56	64	71
Weightlifting: light, free weight, Nautilus	59	68	77	86
Weightlifting: vigorous, free weight, Nautilus	117	135	153	171

Moderate-intensity activities include many things you may already be doing regularly such as yard work, going out to get the mail, or washing the car. Everything counts, and when it all adds up to thirty minutes or more over the course of the day, regularly, you can experience substantial health benefits. It isn't difficult to just get up and move around whenever you have the chance to do so and to choose more strenuous alternatives when you have them available, such as walking up the stairs instead of taking the elevator, or when shopping, parking your car some distance from your destination and walking the rest of the way.[9]

The main issue is not what you choose to do, but that you do *something*. And when you just get started, you'll find that your energy levels, your optimism, and your outlook on life—as well as your physical health—will begin to greatly improve. As Dr. David Sobel states:

> The image and standard of vigorous, sweat-soaked exercise has discouraged many sedentary individuals from even trying to become more active. The bulk of benefit may come from expending as little as 500 calories as week in moderate physical exercise. And such activity need not be an arduous bout of exercise, but can be pleasurable, enjoyable activities: talking, gardening, bowling, dancing, golf, and so on.[10]

To get the most benefit from whatever exercise routine you choose, you have to find out specifically what works for you, which may be different from what everybody else is doing. Most of all, it should be enjoyable and challenging, but not so difficult that it discourages you before you even get started.

A GOOD NIGHT'S SLEEP

In addition to getting enough exercise, a good night's sleep cannot be overrated when it comes to living a happy, healthy life.

If you are not getting enough sleep, then you have a lot in common with about seventy million Americans. Each year more than fifteen hundred Americans die in an estimated one hundred thousand automobile accidents that are attributed to drowsy driving. Thousands of industrial and other work-related accidents result from drowsiness. Even when no accidents occur, workers who are always tired have trouble concentrating, are not as good at problem solving, make more mistakes, and forget more important matters than their peers.

Many serious medical conditions seem related to lack of sleep, though it is not clear whether lack of sleep is the cause or the effect in some of these:

- High blood pressure
- Heart failure, heart attacks, and strokes
- Obesity
- Depression, mood disorders, and other types of mental impairment[11]

Not only does lack of sleep affect you physically, but it also makes it difficult to manage stress, relate well to other people, and maintain a positive outlook on life.

A ZZZZZ'S QUIZZZZZZ

Check any of the following that are true of you:

☐ Most nights, I do not get more than five or six hours of sleep.

☐ Quite often when I'm driving, I have to fight to stay awake.

☐ I often wake up during the night, and when I do, it's hard to fall asleep again.

☐ I sometimes have a hard time staying awake and alert at work.

☐ It is hard for me to concentrate for very long.

☐ I seldom feel refreshed in the morning.

☐ Even if I'm tired, I sometimes have a hard time falling asleep.

☐ I'm not as good at solving problems as I used to be.

☐ I often need a stiff drink, a sleeping pill, or some other substance in order to fall asleep.

☐ I need caffeine to get myself going in the morning and keep myself going during the day.

☐ Sometimes when I wake up at night, I feel as if I'm gasping for air.

This ZZZZZS's quiz is not a scientific tool by any means, but if you checked three or more of these, you should probably consult your physician.

SIMPLE SUGGESTIONS FOR A
STRESS-FREE EXERCISE ROUTINE

Stretching improves your flexibility. When Dave's father was seventy-five, he described for us a daily stretching regime that he has followed for more than twenty years:

These exercises focus mainly on the upper body. I have found them to be excellent for maintaining flexibility in the hands and arms and keeping affected muscles firm. The neck and head exercises improve freedom of movement, and as a result, awareness and reaction time in case of driving emergencies. They also offer a sense of well-being and mental sharpness. The body turning and bending exercises involving the lower body help prevent back pain and muscle spasms. Another benefit that I have experienced is that these exercises seem to help in maintaining very good digestive regularity. The total time to complete this routine is approximately ten minutes. I have found that it makes my day better to preface these exercises with a Scripture reading of two chapters and a time of prayer and reflection.

1. Standing straight, bring arms up from the side and extend to chest level. Swing horizontally to side at the same level and return back down to side. Repeat ten times.

2. From arms at side, raise them forward to shoulder level and hold briefly before lowering them to the side again. Repeat ten times.

3. From arms at side, raise them to stretch position above head; hold briefly and return to side. Repeat ten times.

4. Standing straight, turn head as far as possible to left and right alternately, with slight pause at each position. Repeat five times. Then lift head as high as possible, stretching the chin and neck gently; lower head till chin touches chest, pausing briefly at each position. Repeat five times.

5. Standing straight, fling arms straight out at shoulder level while simultaneously opening and closing fists for finger mobility; return to shoulder level. Repeat ten times.

6. Starting with arms extended to side, bring arms across chest to opposite side and return to original position. (This should be done with vigor.) Repeat ten times.

7. Repeat head and neck exercises as described in #4.

8. With arms extended to side, rotate in windmill motion along side. Repeat ten times.

9. While opening and closing fists, extend arms rapidly outward, alternating right and left as if hitting imaginary punching bag. Do ten times each side.

10. Standing straight, turn upper body alternately to left and right as far as possible, keeping lower body stationary. Do ten times each to left and right.

11. With arms at side, alternately lift arms directly overhead as if reaching for ceiling. Repeat ten times.

12. Deep breathing—lift arms to the front while at the same time inhaling as much air as possible; slowly release the air as arms return to side. Repeat ten times.

13. Using nearby wall or door for support, slowly swing legs out and up as far as possible. Bend knees in swinging action. Repeat five times for each leg.

14. Standing straight with lower body stationary, reach down and touch toes, returning to standing position after each alternating touch. Repeat ten times each side.[12]

Aerobic exercises work your heart and lungs. The possibilities for aerobic exercise are almost endless: You can run or jog, take an aerobic dance class, skip rope, jog in place, ride a bike, swim, or even speed walk. If you have the equipment, you can work out on a Nordic ski machine, a treadmill, a stationary bike, a rowing machine, or a stair step machine.

Lifting light weights repetitively strengthens and conditions your musculoskeletal system—your muscles, tendons, bones, and ligaments—improving muscle tone and endurance. Strength training can also improve your self-esteem, confidence, and sense of self-worth. You don't necessarily have to use barbells or dumbbells in order to increase your muscle tone and strength, though these are specifically designed for this purpose. You can achieve similar results through the regular use of resistance products from a variety of products using anything from rubber straps all the way up to a Bowflex home gym.

Here are some simple suggestions for getting a good night's sleep, collected and condensed from various sources:[13]

1. If you often wake up sore or stiff, or if your bed sags and makes noise every time you move on it, an investment in a higher quality bed and box spring is step one.

2. Avoid alcohol close to bedtime. While it may make you feel drowsy, many people wake up during the night (as the alcohol wears off), unable to fall asleep again. Perhaps more importantly, alcohol and other substances can interfere with the deeper stages of sleep, called REM sleep,[14] during which dreaming occurs.

3. Try to go to bed around the same time each night. Your body and mind have certain rhythms that have been established over time. Keeping your sleeping and rising routine within these rhythms contributes to your health.

4. Avoid things that might upset you just before turning out the lights. For example, many people watch the late night news while lying in bed, then mull over the bad news while they lie there in the dark staring at the ceiling, when the morning news will be pretty much the same in a few hours' time. The same could be said for watching potentially disturbing videos or even reading books or magazines that are negatively stimulating. If you read in bed, read something relaxing and peaceful.

5. Keep the room dark, or at least as dark as possible. Control outside noises using white noise, relaxing soft sounds, or even earplugs. Keep the temperature between

sixty and seventy degrees. If you like it on the colder side, you might consider wearing socks to bed.

6. Limit your intake of food and liquids, especially caffeinated drinks, just prior to retiring. If you drink fluids after 6:00 p.m., there's a good chance you will need to get up during the night to relieve your bladder. Sugars or grain-related products can hinder your sleep. Fruits or berries or protein-based snacks are OK as long as they are not eaten too close to bedtime. Spicy foods or other foods to which you are sensitive may interfere with your sleep.

7. Exercise in the morning, if possible. If you must exercise in the evening, try to give your body a chance to slow down again before bedtime.

8. If you tend to wake up and then stare at the clock, find a way to keep the alarm on but the clock's face out of sight in order to decrease your anxiety over when it's going to ring or if you'll hear it when it does.

9. If you happen to wake up and your mind goes into overdrive about your problems or issues, write them down in a small notebook that you keep nearby for this purpose; you can also write down what you plan to do about them tomorrow. This may relieve your conscious mind of trying to remember everything when daylight comes. Then, after you awake, go through your list and cross off those things that seemed so very important during the night but are not so important now. Do what you can about the rest.

Each night, as much as possible, let your last waking thoughts be something like this:

Dear Lord, I've done what I could today, and I'll do what I can tomorrow to do what is left undone right now. I'll need Your help then as I did today to make the best decisions and the most reasonable and responsible plans for the future that I may need to make. But for right now, Lord, I leave all of it—yesterday, today, and tomorrow—in Your hands because I know I can trust You with it while I sleep. Amen.

And then, maybe often, you'll hear Him whisper: "Come to me, all you who are weary and burdened, and I will give you rest" (Matt. 11:28).

So…what's your plan? Write it here.

My Plan

Three things I will do today to improve my exercise and rest:

1. _____

2. _____

3. _____

Three things I will try to do within the next three months to continue this improvement:

1. _____

2. _____

3. _____

SIMPLE HEALTH

Three things I will try to do within the next six months to turn these improvements into habits:

1. _____

2. _____

3. _____

Today's date: _____ / _____ / _____

Chapter 5

Eat and Drink Healthy Things
The Decision to Make Nutritious Choices

Let food be thy medicine, and medicine be thy food.
—HIPPOCRATES (460–380 B.C.)

Maintaining healthy nutritional habits is one of the best ways to foster a lifestyle of wellness—on that, most Americans would agree. Mentally, we assent to the claim of Hippocrates that food can be "medicine" to our bodies—that what we eat has a profound affect on our bodies' health as well as our enjoyment of life. However, each individual's interpretation of "medicinal food" varies on whether we view it as healing our bodies or as "comfort" for our wounded spirits.

I (Dave) vividly recall my visit to the operating room of a good friend and heart surgeon. It was sobering to watch his assistant cradle the patient's unbeating heart in her hands while the surgeon did four bypasses in less than an hour. Equally unforgettable was watching my friend clean a plug of light yellow, waxy plaque from the obese patient's left carotid artery (the main blood supply to his brain on that side), which was almost totally blocked. I had heard of plaque, but I had never seen it up close. Without a doubt, the patient was fortunate to still be around because he saw my surgeon-friend before the blockage resulted in a stroke. Too often people fail to be responsible for taking care of their bodies, and then they blame others for their demise.

SIMPLE HEALTH

On March 10, 2004, the U.S. House of Representatives passed a measure known as the "Cheeseburger Bill." This particular bill was designed to protect the fast-food industry from potential frivolous lawsuits filed by, you guessed it, overweight customers.

Today, many Americans are similarly at risk without even knowing it due to our high-fat, high-cholesterol, additive-riddled diets comprised primarily of processed and manufactured foods. The good news is that each person has the power to make smart, nutritious choices when it comes to eating and, as a result, lead a more productive life.

HOW DID WE GET SO BIG?

The fact that we are overfed should be obvious enough. All you have to do is look around the next time you go shopping or to a restaurant, noting the number of obese individuals waddling around. And we're not speaking of adults, here. Our children are also increasingly overweight, a trend that is disturbing because "junk food" habits formed early are hard to break,[1] and fat lodged in various places in childhood is difficult to displace any time later. In fact, there is such an epidemic of obesity in children today that a March 2005 report in the *New England Journal of Medicine* predicted that their lives will be less healthy and *shorter* than the lives of their parents.[2]

In the Middle Ages, one's girth was linked to one's worth, and starving peasants envied the corpulence of their lords and ladies. Until relatively recently, obesity was not taken that seriously. However, the World Health Organization (WHO) currently estimates that, globally, there are more than one *billion* overweight adults, at least *three hundred million* of them obese.[3] In July 2004, the U.S. Department of Health and Human Services (HHS) made a major policy shift by removing language in Medicare regulations that stated that obesity was not an illness, thus making it possible for Medicare patients to receive medical treatment for obesity.

According to the most recent data available at the time of this writing, in the United States:

- Sixty-four percent of adults twenty years of age and older are either overweight or obese. (See the note for definitions.[4]) This number has increased by 18 percent since 1980.

- Thirty-one percent of adults twenty years of age and older are obese. This number has more than doubled in the last twenty years.

- Fifteen percent of adolescents between the ages of twelve and nineteen are overweight.

- Fifteen percent of children between the ages of six and eleven are overweight. The percentage of children and adolescents who are defined as overweight has more than doubled in the past thirty years.

Being overweight or obese is significantly associated with:

- Type-2 (adult onset) diabetes
- Cardiovascular disease (CVD)
- High blood pressure
- Stroke
- High cholesterol
- Asthma
- Arthritis
- Certain forms of cancer
- Poor health status in general[5]

If we want to make changes to improve our quality of life, we need to begin with what we eat, which starts with what we put in the grocery cart.

HEALTHY SHOPPING IS THE FIRST STEP

For many food products, multiple choices are available in most grocery stores. Health-conscious consumers make healthier shopping choices. Some brands listed below may not be available where you shop, but the key is to read the labels and compare ingredients in order to identify the healthier brands. Be wary of the following terms: enriched, refined, or fortified. The basic principles include: choose whole foods free of herbicides or pesticides, hormones or antibiotics, additives, preservatives, refined sugars, salts, artificial sweetening, caffeine, coloring or flavoring, hydrogenated or partially hydrogenated oils (trans fats), hydrolyzed vegetable protein, nitrates, nitrites, and MSG.[6]

Our friend Toni Olson is a health educator whose passion is helping parents understand how to provide optimal nutrition for their families. This is Toni's guide to buying healthy groceries:

SHOPPER'S GUIDE		
FOOD	**BRAND**	**COMMENTS**
Applesauce	Leroux Creek	Organic, gluten free with delicious berry blends
	Motts Natural	Contains only apples, water, and ascorbic acid
	Santa Cruz Organic	Certified organic, variety of blends
Bars	Larabars	Better than most
	Nature Valley	No trans fats
Bread	Alvarado St. Bakery	No pesticides/herbicides, chemical fertilizers, genetically modified organisms (GMOs), artificial ingredients, preservatives, or trans fats. Buy 100 percent whole-grain breads or try sprouted grains.
	French Meadows Bakery	

FOOD	BRAND	COMMENTS
	Rudi's Organic	
	Nature's Own Whole Wheat	Also good. More natural choices are available in the health food section
Cereal	Mother's Peace Cereal	There are many brands of great-tasting cereals that contain organic ingredients, natural sweeteners (no refined sugar, aspartame, Splenda), no hydrogenated oils, and minimal flavorings, preservatives, etc.
	Nature Valley	
	Kashi	
	Nature's Path Instant Oatmeal	
Dairy	Nest Fresh Eggs	Organic, free-range chicken eggs that contain more nutrition with no hormones, antibiotics, toxic pesticides
	Horizon Milk, Cheese, and Butter	Organic milk with no hormones, antibiotics
	Royal Crest Delivery	Also good quality
Deli meats	Applegate Farms	Their meats and cheeses contain no colorings, flavorings, etc.
	Boar's Head	You can also get nitrate-free oven-roasted turkey from most deli counters.
Flour	Whole grain	Try whole wheat, spelt, rice, oat bran, amaranth, etc.
Fruits and vegetables	Organic	Buy organic fruits and vegetables when they are available. When they aren't available, soak soft-skinned fruits and veggies in a mix of 1 gallon water to 1 tablespoon sea salt or vinegar for five minutes to remove the pesticide residue

SIMPLE HEALTH

FOOD	BRAND	COMMENTS
Juice	Northland, Hansen	100 percent real fruit juice without added sugars
	Juicy Juice	
	R. W. Knudsen	
Macaroni and cheese	Annie's Organic	
	Simply Organic	Just five ingredients of real food. Organic without added artificial flavorings, colorings, preservatives, and chemicals.
Meats	Maverick Farms	We buy only organic meat. Smaller portions of leaner, healthier meats without the hormones, antibiotics, and poor animal conditions are very important for a healthy diet.
Nut butters	Adam's	
	Arrowhead Mills	Just real peanuts. Turn jar upside down in your pantry to keep the oil off the top. Have kids grind their own at the store (Vitamin, Maranatha, Cottage, Wild Oats, Whole Foods).
Popcorn	Your own!	You can pop popcorn in a paper bag in the microwave with canola oil. Or use an air popper. Sprinkle some Herbamare seasonings or coconut flakes on it.
Potato chips	Boulder Chips	Contain no preservatives, additives, artificial colors, or hydrogenated oils. Read the ingredients on "flavored" chips as these may contain some questionable flavorings, including MSG.
	Guiltless Gourmet	

FOOD	BRAND	COMMENTS
	Lay's Natural	
Potstickers	Ling Lings	No harmful ingredients. Easy, pretty healthy, and kids love them.
Salt	Sea salt	Salt in its natural form is much better for you!
Sugar	Sucanat	Great replacement for refined sugar; hasn't gone through as much processing. Can be used as a 1:1 substitute for white sugar in baking.
Sweeteners	Stevia	Concentrated natural sweetener. Great in coffee, tea, etc. Stevia is a slow-release sweetener and helps maintain even blood sugar levels. Please avoid artificial sweeteners, as their safety is open to question.
Waffles	Vans	Delicious without the artificial ingredients, hydrogenated oils, and preservatives.
	Lifestream	
Yogurt	Stoneyfield Farms	Organic yogurt that contains natural sweeteners. Sugar content of this yogurt is much less than others.
	Mountain High	
	Redwood Hills	
	Goat yogurt	

Organic farming differs from conventional farming in the methods used to grow crops. Where traditional farmers apply chemical fertilizers to the soil to grow their crops, organic farmers feed and build soil with natural fertilizer. Traditional farmers use insecticides to get rid of insects and disease, while organic farmers use natural methods such as insect predators and barriers for this purpose. Traditional farmers control weed growth by applying synthetic herbicides, but organic farmers use crop rotation, tillage, hand weeding, cover crops, and mulches to control weeds. The result is that conventionally grown food is often tainted with chemical residues, which can be harmful to humans. The following foods tend to be higher in pesticide levels: Fruits—peaches, apples, strawberries, nectarines, pears, cherries, red raspberries, imported grapes. Vegetables—bell peppers, spinach, celery, potatoes, hot peppers. These foods tend to be lower in pesticide levels: Fruits—pineapples, plantains, mangoes, bananas, watermelon, plums, kiwi fruit, blueberries, papaya, grapefruit. Vegetables—avocado, cauliflower, brussels sprouts, asparagus, radishes, broccoli, onions, okra, cabbage, eggplant.[7]

THE TEN COMMANDMENTS OF EATING AND DRINKING HEALTHY

Fortunately, you don't have to be a rocket scientist to figure out that the weight problem of most Americans is caused by the fact that we eat *too much* of the *wrong things*. And it doesn't take a degree in nutrition to know what the "right foods" are for you to eat—fruits, vegetables, lean meats, less sugar, and less processed foods. Most importantly, these foods should be eaten in smaller, healthier amounts—and that will help you lose weight more effectively than any fad diet that will ever come on the market.

To help you get started, here are what we like to call "The Ten Commandments of a Healthy Diet." These are practical suggestions to show you where to begin:

1. Eat, drink, and be merry. Accentuate the positive. The Lord put food on this earth for us to enjoy. So lose the anxiety, go "back to the garden" (as in the Garden of Eden), and consume a variety of healthy foods daily from

all of the food groups (including adequate amounts of fiber). Don't forget to be thankful for all of the good things that God gives you.

2. Eat a healthy breakfast every day. Many breakfast cereals contain significant amounts of fiber. Breakfast eaters perform better at work or school and find it easier to control their weight, since a good breakfast jump-starts your metabolism after your overnight fast.

3. Drink about one-half ounce of pure water per pound of your weight per day, 15 percent more when you exercise. If you are new to good hydration, increase from your current intake toward your goal slowly.

4. Eat at least nine servings of vegetables, fruits, and whole grains—whole, pesticide- and herbicide-free—daily. Variety is essential—i.e., three servings of broccoli is not as healthful as one serving of broccoli, one of legumes, and one of berries.

5. Consume several small amounts of lean protein daily, versus consuming large amounts at one sitting. Some people find that eating small healthy meals up to five or six times a day can help combat their cravings for foods that are unhealthy. Vegetarians should be careful to consume enough high-quality protein, including leucine, an amino acid essential to developing lean muscle and regulating hormones related to appetite and metabolism.

6. If you drink alcohol, stick to red wine, and no more than two servings per day. If you're pregnant, do not drink alcohol *at all*, since even a single drink may cause brain damage to your developing child.[8] You can drink grape juice if you want to benefit from the health benefits of the antioxidants in the grapes.

7. Keep healthy snacks handy. Almonds, cashews, pecans, or walnuts provide fiber, vitamin E, and monounsaturated fats. They are "heart healthy" but high in calories, so use moderation. Note for chocolate lovers: A *small amount* of the right kind of dark chocolate (Dove Dark Chocolate) can be a health-enhancing reward, due to the type of flavonoids in it.[9]

8. Avoid most processed foods, especially those containing refined sugar or flour, excess salts, unnecessary fats, MSG, trans fats, and other additives. These are most prevalent in cake mixes, cereal and energy bars, chips and crackers, dried soups, fast food, frozen entrees, margarine, nondairy creamers and whipped toppings, packaged cookies and candy, packaged doughnuts, pies, and cakes. Think "natural" versus "manufactured."

9. Skip the junk—go for quality. Ban sugar-loaded soft drinks, candy, and other calorie-dense but nutrition-deficient "foods" from your house. Nobody can snack on what is not available. Forget "fast food" and "TV dinners" and stick to "slow" food that you can enjoy with your family around your dining room table (or wherever you normally eat together) as often as possible. This fellowship will build quality relationships and enhance spiritual connections with each other.

10. Become an informed consumer. Know what you are eating and where it came from (i.e., how it was raised or cultivated, plus what its benefits or dangers may be to your health and the health of those you love). Read the labels, read the labels, read the labels. This is one of the most important factors.

11. Bonus commandment—know why you want to practice better nutrition. Ask yourself: *What is my deepest*

*motivation for wanting to learn about and practice better
nutrition for my family and me?* If your answer is: "So
we all lose weight and look great," or "So we can avoid
a bunch of doctor bills," or "So my spouse won't have
a heart attack," over the long term you probably won't
change much about what you or your family eat and
drink. Long-term change requires better motivation, and
the only motive that will sustain you will be: "Because
I believe that we are here for a purpose, and in order to
fulfill it, we all need to achieve optimal health."

AVOID THE "FAD DIET" CRAZE

You've most likely seen this flyer, stapled to a telephone pole: *"Lose
30 Pounds in 30 Days—for 30 Dollars, Guaranteed."*

It's clever advertising and very tempting. If you really could lose
a pound a day and reach your ideal weight in a relatively short time,
that means that you can delay the diet for a while. In other words,
you can keep living the way you are living and still shed that excess
weight by beach weather, or that next college reunion, or whatever is
on the calendar for which you would want to look fit and trim.

But notice that the flyer doesn't say "thirty pounds of *fat.*" The
reason being that although most people can lose weight on any diet
that restricts calories, no matter what you do or how hard you work
at it, the most *fat* you will likely lose on a reasonable diet is one
pound per week.

Fortunately, if you're really interested, we have a diet just right
for you—and that is eating the simple, nutritious foods we just dis-
cussed. In fact, this is usually the best diet that ends up working for
most people, long term—specifically because it's a reasonable diet
that they will actually put into practice. The best diet for anyone
is one that they will both *employ* and *enjoy,* for eating is one of the
greatest pleasures of life, a gift from God, who designed us with taste
buds when He could just as well not have done so. His perspective
on "dieting" would be that our goal should be to reach and maintain

optimal health. Reasonable weight loss might be a side effect of this process for those who are currently overweight, and if so, it's a side effect that could last a lifetime.

Achieving optimal health involves all the arenas of life that this book is about—biological, psychological, sociological, and spiritual. *Biologically*, we need to understand and practice good nutrition—eat and drink healthy things in moderation. *Psychologically*, we need to get past emotional challenges such as addictions to food and drink (including alcohol), cravings, and a self-image that will only be satisfactory when our body looks like the body of someone else. *Sociologically*, we need to get back to the family dining room table, where enjoying the meal and conversation was something of a health-enhancing ritual that's been lost since the advent of TV dinners. Our endeavor to make these changes will likely be more successful if we establish alliances with others whose support we need, as they need ours. *Spiritually*, we can expect encouragement from God's Spirit and supernatural strength to achieve any goal we choose that is fully aligned with His will.

WHAT'S YOUR MOTIVATION?

The problem with most "diets" is not so much that they are "fads," but that their focus is negative—losing weight; counting cholesterol; knowing the RDAs; deciphering labels; computing calories and carbohydrates; worrying over fats, sugar, or sodium; weighing your portions; and so forth. It's to the point where you have a full-fledged case of diet anxiety. The net result for many is that, once they've overstepped the restraints of whatever diet they're on, they binge or relapse—the end being worse than the beginning.

Is your primary motivation for losing weight or considering a diet negative or positive? Here's how our friend John replied when we asked his opinion on why he might want to start a diet:

1. I can't find the pliers to zip up my pants.

2. I was standing on the street corner when a cop came up and said, "Hey, you two, break it up!"

3. I was sunbathing and people started shouting, "Beached whale! Beached whale!"

4. I have to use two hands to fasten my seat belt.

5. I have to fly first class because I cannot fit in a coach seat.

6. My primary form of recreation is making sandwiches.

7. I do not own a pair of tie shoes.

8. My best friend's idea of a practical joke is a talking toilet seat that yells, "For the love of God, get off of me!"

9. I can name more than thirty varieties of cheese.

10. When I eat a salad to better my health, I reward myself by using an entire bottle of blue cheese dressing.

Seriously, check all of the following motives that apply to you if you're dieting or considering doing so:

☐ I want to lose weight.

☐ I want to feel better about myself.

☐ I want to stay as "young" as I can for as long as I can.

☐ I want to look more attractive.

☐ What I eat is one thing in life that I can control.

☐ I want to get ahead in life, and overweight people have it that much harder.

☐ I want to stay in the "healthy" category, in terms of health and life insurance.

☐ I want to avoid weight-related chronic illnesses.

☐ I want to be healthier and improve my quality of life.

SIMPLE HEALTH

☐ I want to be able to serve the Lord as long as possible.

Many people will check three to five of these reasons, but we suspect that for believers, unless their motives include the final option, their attempts to diet will fail over time. Ninety percent of people who lose weight end up gaining it back because they have not made what they consume part of their belief system, lifestyle, and spiritual identity—who they are in relation to the Lord. When we're moving toward God's purpose for our lives, this can produce sustained behavioral change. This is why successful dieting really involves a spiritual transformation for many people. In a real sense, you are serving God by your choices of food and drink, including the amounts involved. Doing anything to excess of what is healthy for the body interferes with God's purpose for our lives and our ability (especially our physical ability) to carry out our destiny, as defined by Him.[10]

RAISING HEALTHY KIDS

As we noted earlier in this chapter, childhood obesity has reached epidemic proportions. Any parent or caregiver who is concerned about keeping his or her child healthy will want practical ways to get the child to make nutritious food choices. Here are a few tips that our friend Toni suggests to encourage your child to eat healthy:

- Have fruit washed and easily available.

- Cut up vegetables and have them ready to eat. Keep them in disposable plastic bags visibly placed on the bottom shelf of the fridge.

- Use fruit for a sweet snack.

- Cut up fruit and vegetables in fun shapes and send them as a snack in packed lunches.

- Serve fruit and vegetables with a variety of delicious dipping sauces as a snack at home.

- Serve salads first at dinnertime, when kids are hungriest.

- Try new fruit and vegetables—don't assume your kids won't like them. Choose a variety of colors. (Sometimes a child needs to be exposed to a new food fourteen times before he or she will eat it.)

- "Pulverize and disguise" your vegetables, adding them to soups, pasta, eggs, burritos, and so forth.

- Have your kids help plant seeds and grow a vegetable garden.

- Make smoothies loaded with a variety of fruits (strawberries, blueberries, pineapple, and bananas).

- Give your kids concentrated fruit and vegetable snack foods, without artificial ingredients.

In addition to these tips, here are some healthy snacks that you can reach for when you have the "munchies":

HEALTHY SNACKS	
Raw veggie strips (cucumber, jicama, bell peppers, cauliflower, tomatoes, broccoli, zucchini spears)	Fruit kabobs (kiwi, melon, mango, pineapple, plums, pears, strawberries, blueberries, papaya, orange sections)
Celery with nut butter and raisins	Hard-boiled eggs
Sugar snap peas	Olives
Hummus and carrots	Guacamole with baked corn chips
Popcorn seasoned with herbs	Popcorn sprinkled with Parmesan cheese

Pretzels with nut butters (almond, peanut, cashew)	Pita or English muffin pizzas with strips of bell peppers and olives
Dried figs	Cottage cheese with applesauce
Plain yogurt with applesauce or fresh fruit	Smoothies with flax seeds and fruit
Edamame	Turkey jerky (low sodium; no MSG)
Homemade muffins with ground flax meal and nuts	Homemade muesli (rolled oats with nuts, seeds, dried fruit, etc.)
Rice pudding	Sesame seed bars
Zucchini pancakes	Zucchini bread
Homemade snack mix with cereals, pretzels, nuts, dried fruit	Black bean salsa with baked corn chips
Apple slices with cinnamon	Chickpea pate
Yam chips	Baked sweet potato chunks
Raw nuts (macadamia, pistachios, sunflower seeds, pecans, almonds, walnuts, Brazil nuts, cashews)	Raw seeds (pumpkin, sunflower)
Homemade frozen juice pops	Calbee Snapea Crisps
Refried beans with sprouted grain tortillas	Fruit-juice sweetened cookies
Spelt sesame sticks	Marinated mushrooms
Brown rice with vanilla soymilk and 1 teaspoon maple syrup	Brown rice heated and served with Bragg's liquid aminos
Roasted soy nuts	Organic food bars
Larabars	Rebars
Sliced turkey rolled with asparagus inside	Whole-wheat pasta salad with tuna, olives, and chopped tomatoes
Cheddar Guppies (healthier version of Goldfish)	Rice crackers with olive tapenade or kidney bean spread
Terra Taro Chips	Concentrated fruit and vegetable snacks

So, what's your plan—in terms of consuming healthy food and drink in moderation?

My Plan

In the next month, I will:

1. _____

2. _____

3. _____

Within three months, I will:

1. _____

2. _____

3. _____

Long-term, I will:

1. _____

2. _____

3. _____

Chapter 6

Take Charge of Your Health

Learn How to Be Proactive in Preventing Disease

> Medical care accounts for only 10 percent of all our
> health outcomes, and the way we live determines the
> other 90 percent.[1]
>
> —Dr. Richard Palmer, Past President, AMA

Some people believe providers of medical and dental care or various government agencies are responsible for their health care, but that is only part of the truth. The other side involves individuals taking a proactive stance in maintaining good health.

This chapter, which is divided into two sections—prevention and treatment—is going to give you different ideas to take control of your own health. Don't be overwhelmed. In reality, it is likely that you are already doing many of them. But grab a pencil and highlight those suggestions that seem to make the most sense for you to start working on today.

AN OUNCE OF PREVENTION

Benjamin Franklin said, "An ounce of prevention is worth a pound of cure." This applies perhaps more to health than to any other area of life.

SIMPLE HEALTH

Chronic diseases—such as heart disease, cancer, and diabetes—are the leading causes of death and disability in the United States. These diseases account for seven of every ten deaths and affect the quality of life of ninety million Americans. According to the Centers for Disease Control and Prevention (CDC), Americans are sick a total of more than *four billion* days annually; each year, Americans spend more than $950 *billion* on direct medical costs. Although chronic diseases are among the most common and costly health problems, they are also among the most preventable. Adopting healthy behaviors such as eating nutritious foods, being physically active, and avoiding tobacco use can prevent or control the devastating effects of these diseases.[2]

Part of taking prevention seriously also involves taking measures to control health-threatening things in your environment, starting with your home.

"Mind if I smoke?"

Secondhand smoke contains more than four thousand chemicals and at least sixty known carcinogens. According to one Mayo Clinic report, some of the components found in tobacco smoke that are suspected or known to be carcinogenic include formaldehyde, arsenic, cadmium, benzene, and ethylene oxide. Other detrimental things in tobacco smoke include ammonia, carbon monoxide, methanol, hydrogen cyanide, and nicotine. "In 1992, the Environmental Protection Agency classified environmental tobacco smoke in the most dangerous category of cancer-causing agents," the report says.[3]

Secondhand smoke is linked to cancers of the lung, breast, cervix, and bladder. Experts believe that secondhand smoke is to blame for roughly three thousand lung cancer deaths in nonsmokers each year in the United States. Some research indicates that people exposed to a spouse's cigarette smoke for several decades are about 20 percent more likely to have lung cancer. Those who are exposed long-term to secondhand smoke in the workplace or social settings may increase their risk of lung cancer by about 25 percent.

The report also cited a 1999 U.S. Surgeon General's statement that secondhand smoke increased cardiovascular risks in general and was associated with sixty-two thousand deaths annually from heart disease caused by narrowing of the blood vessels of the heart.[4]

This situation would be serious enough if it only involved consenting adults, but it's far more serious when it injures children. An infant whose mother smokes is 38 percent more likely to be hospitalized during the first year of life; for infants with two smoking parents the number is over 50 percent.[5] Children with a smoking parent are 60 percent more likely to have a buildup of fluid in the middle ear, which can lead to ear infections—the most common cause of hospitalization in children.[6] There is a growing body of evidence linking secondhand smoke to Sudden Infant Death Syndrome. One study found that adult leukemia was significantly associated with exposure to maternal smoking before the age of ten. In addition, the Environmental Protection Agency (EPA) estimates that up to one million children have aggravated asthma symptoms due to secondhand smoke.[7]

So the next time someone asks, "Mind if I smoke?", you should feel free to reply, "Yes, I do mind, for two reasons. First, I hate to see you hurting yourself, because I like you and want to have you around. Second, scientific evidence has shown that secondhand smoke is harmful, and I want to do everything in my power to prevent things from harming me and those I love."

Other toxins

Many potentially harmful toxins find their way into your home in smaller amounts through a variety of means, including the air, dirt that is tracked in, building materials, insecticides and pesticides, paints, solvents, and some cleaning materials. These toxins may include arsenic, ammonia, asbestos, benzene, chlorine bleach, dioxin, formaldehyde, lead, or mercury. While your exposure may seem miniscule, what is the point of unnecessarily exposing yourself or your family to things that might hurt them? Here are some suggestions for limiting your exposure:

1. Avoid solvents or unprotected contact with solvents. Solvents are contained in gasoline, rubbing alcohol, glues, adhesives, paint thinners, some cleaning solutions, and some cosmetics. Most dry cleaning is done by using toxic solvents. Use nontoxic cleaning products, or make your own with substances such as soda, soap, and vinegar.[8]

2. Use solid woods and natural, untreated fabrics—bonded wood products, particleboard, plywood, and synthetic carpeting or upholstery can release toxic fumes. If something smells "new," the scent is most likely from toxic fumes. Safer flooring is hardwood, stone, tile, or marble with nontoxic grout and sealant. Note: houseplants like aloe vera, elephant's ear, English ivy, and peace lily can help remove toxins like formaldehyde and benzene from the air.[9]

3. To reduce the risk from pesticides, do not handle or use chemical tick and flea collars or flea dips on your pets. Use natural products—as much as possible—to control insects in your garden since many over-the-counter sprays can be toxic, whether consumed or airborne. If you use a commercial pest control service, ensure that their sprays and other means of pest control are nontoxic to humans.[10]

4. Avoid using any product that contains lead. If your house has lead paint, have it professionally removed. Note: If you plan to plant a vegetable garden, test the soil for lead. If lead is present, remove at least the first six inches and cover with lead-free topsoil.[11]

Indoor air pollution

Around the world, people are increasingly concerned about "sick-house syndrome." According to the EPA, indoor air pollution may be two to five times worse than outdoor air pollution. The EPA lists indoor air pollution as one of the top five public health risks. This is troubling since people spend approximately 90 percent of their time indoors.[12]

Most homes have more than one source that contributes to indoor air pollution. The cumulative effect of these sources can present a serious risk. Everyday household items such as cleaning supplies emit volatile organic compounds (VOCs), which have been blamed for symptoms such as eye, nose, and throat irritation; headaches; skin irritation; shortness of breath; and fatigue.[13] Since these symptoms are similar to those of colds and other viral diseases, it is often difficult to determine if the symptoms are from indoor air pollutants. Long-term health effects, including some respiratory diseases, heart disease, and cancer, may show up either years after exposure has occurred or only after long or repeated periods of exposure.[14]

You can improve your home's air quality by:

- Cleaning air conditioners, humidifiers, dehumidifiers, and heat exchangers regularly.

- Fitting your gas range with a hood fan that vents air pollutants to the outside. If this is not possible, keep the window open and use a window exhaust fan while cooking. Have your gas or oil company regularly inspect your furnace, gas water heater, or gas clothes dryer.

- Venting kerosene or gas heaters to the outside of your home. Don't use your gas oven to heat your home.

- Never cooking inside your home with anything that creates carbon monoxide.

- Installing detectors for smoke, carbon monoxide, and radon gas in appropriate places in your home. Each of these could save your life.

- Opening the fireplace damper before lighting a fire and keeping it open until the ashes are cool.

- Making sure wood or coal stoves are vented to the outside and that their exhaust systems don't leak.

- Using only nontoxic cleaners.

- Burning only nonpetroleum candles with cloth wicks.[15]

- Using safe paint—paint without harmful VOCs.

Allergens

The four most common household allergens are dust mites, pollen, pet dander, and mold. Dust mites are microscopic bugs (smaller than the period at the end of this sentence) that thrive in warm and humid places such as beds, upholstered furniture, and carpets. They live on skin cells shed by humans and pets.[16] Their fecal material contributes to asthma and some allergies. Try the following to reduce your exposure to dust mites:

- Wash bedding weekly in hot water. Dry on high to kill any mites that survived their bath.

- Use antiallergenic encasements for bedding, including pillows, mattresses, comforters, and box springs.

- Bedsheets should be 100 percent cotton, and pillows should be stuffed with 100 percent cotton. Invest in organic mattresses. Avoid down pillows or comforters, which offer a haven for dust mites.[17]

- Use upholstery fabrics made from 100 percent organic cotton, hemp, silk, or any other natural fiber. The filling in cushions should be cotton or wool rather than polyurethane foam.

- Vacuum thoroughly using a High Efficiency Particulate Arresting (HEPA) filter vacuum and bags that seal in dust.[18]

- Clean thoroughly once a week using equipment that traps dust rather than releasing it back into the air.

- Filter the air with a HEPA air purifier, which will eliminate 99.7 percent of indoor airborne allergens.

- Dehumidify the air if you live in a humid climate.

- Use HEPA air filters on heating and air conditioning systems.

Pollen collects on hair, clothing, and exposed parts of your body. It can be managed by:

- Avoiding outdoor activities in the morning, especially during high-pollen months.

- Closing all your windows or using filter screens if windows must be opened.

- Removing your shoes before entering your home.

- Showering and washing your hair each night before going to bed.

Dander (pet dandruff) gets into the air when pets groom themselves. Hints for limiting dander's effect on your health include:

- Wiping down indoor surfaces frequently, keeping your pets outdoors as much as possible.

- Vacuuming frequently using a HEPA vacuum cleaner.

- Using a dust mask when cleaning.

- Washing your pet regularly with a dander-reducing shampoo, followed with an antidander spray.

- Washing your hands after touching your pet.

Mold is a common allergen, especially in humid areas such as damp basements, closets, refrigerator drip pans, air conditioners, garbage pails, and shower stalls. To control mold:

- Clean the refrigerator pan every few months.

- Remove visible mold with nontoxic cleaning products.

- Keep the humidity level in your home below 50 percent.

- Use exhaust fans in the kitchen and the bathroom.

- Address water leaks immediately.

Infectious germs

Each year, more than 160,000 people die in the United States with an infectious disease as the underlying cause of death. (Infectious diseases are caused by viruses, bacteria, parasites, and fungi.) The CDC suggests the following seven simple and inexpensive steps for preventing infectious diseases:[19]

1. Wash your hands often. This helps eliminate germs you have picked up from surfaces or animals. Hand washing is particularly important before, during, and after you prepare food; before you eat; and after you use the bathroom.

2. Routinely clean and disinfect surfaces, especially in the kitchen and bathroom. Soap and water, with scrubbing, is usually adequate for cleaning. Disinfecting with bleach or another disinfectant adds a measure of protection.

3. Handle and prepare food safely. Know which foods must be refrigerated. Don't leave perishable food out for more than two hours. Keep cold foods cold; hot foods hot. Don't allow juices from meat, seafood, poultry, or eggs to drip on other foods. Wash raw fruits and vegetables. Cook meats and poultry adequately.

4. Get immunized, and keep your immunizations current. Adults need tetanus and diphtheria boosters every ten years. If you travel, be aware of immunizations needed. Be sure your children are immunized, and keep records for everyone in the family.

5. Use antibiotics appropriately. Colds, flu, and other viruses do not respond to antibiotics. Bacteria can become resistant to treatment if children are given antibiotics when they do not need them.

6. Keep your pets healthy. Keep their immunizations up to date. Don't allow them to use the children's sandbox for their potty.

7. Avoid contact with wild animals, which can carry deadly diseases. Rodents can carry the plague or Hantavirus infection. Ticks transmit Rocky Mountain spotted fever and Lyme disease. Bats, raccoons, skunks, and foxes can transmit rabies.

Noise pollution

Prolonged exposure to noise can cause impaired intellectual performance and learning ability, higher blood pressure, and lowered tolerance of frustration.[20] Noise pollution can come from transportation noise, loud music, loud neighbors, television, appliances, construction noise, or industrial noise. According to a German study, chronic noise exposure can lead to heart attacks. For women, environmental noises were a health hazard. Those who reported annoying environmental noises were 50 percent more likely to have had a heart attack than those who didn't report them. Men weren't affected by environmental noises, but noisy workplaces made them 30 percent more likely to have a heart attack. Studies have suggested that chronic noise exposure causes stress, which leads to increased blood pressure and changes in cholesterol. These changes can contribute to the development of heart disease.[21]

If noise pollution is an issue for you:

- Communicate with family members regarding the noise level in your home. For example, if your husband can't go to sleep without the TV on and you can't go to sleep with it on, work out a compromise.[22]

- Fix noisy appliances and other noise-producing things in your environment.

- Counter irritating noise with soothing sounds: slow, soothing music has been shown to reduce stress.[23]

Ergonomics

The American Society of Interior Designers says that "ergonomics is rapidly emerging as a 'must' for workplace design and home design as well." A good home is designed for efficiency, for comfort, and for the safety of those who live in it. Regardless of the period and style, a healthy home is one that gives one a sense of harmony and purity. Over time, in a healthy home you may notice that you breathe more easily, feel more content, and begin each day with heightened energy and enthusiasm.[24]

The healthy home nurtures those who dwell inside and also protects the world beyond its walls. Designed with sensitivity for the environment, it is energy-efficient, economical, sustainable, and non-polluting. Suggestions include:

- If you have a home office, design it with good ergonomics in mind. Make it adaptable to others in the home if they use it also. Adjustable chairs and tables are a must if both adults and children use it.

- Good lighting is a must in all areas of your home and should be designed for specific tasks in each area.

- Good interior design is a must. Colors should be eye appealing and not distracting, creating a sense of harmony and helping to eliminate stress and strain.

A healthy home should be designed to be "energy efficient" for those who live and work in it, which will help reduce fatigue and allow for more recreational time as a family. A home with plenty of storage, with everything in its place, and where things are organized and not in disarray or cluttered will make for a more organized and less stressful life.

A POUND OF CURE

Of course, disease is not *always* preventable. There may be times when you pay a visit to a physician or a dentist. Even so, you can take charge of your medical or dental health. It's in your power to opt for the best health care by becoming informed of your insurance coverage, including things like co-pays, deductibles, and any limits in terms of your plan's participating physicians, dentists, and treatment facilities.

Managing your dental care

Many people with dental issues put off treatment as long as possible, even though scientific studies have shown a correlation between periodontitis[25] and other diseases. Periodontal bacteria can enter the blood stream, travel to major organs, and begin new infections. These infections can compromise the immune system and weaken the body's ability to eliminate toxicity and to heal. Unfortunately, most physicians don't ask about a patient's dental health when working up a treatment plan for other problems. So it's up to you to be sure that you report your dental issues to your medical doctor. Be sure they are a regular part of your health portfolio.

Schedule a periodontal evaluation if you notice any symptoms of periodontal disease such as bleeding or swollen gums; if you have heart disease, diabetes, respiratory disease or osteoporosis; if you are thinking of becoming pregnant; if you have a family member with periodontal disease; or if you have a sore or irritation in your mouth that doesn't get better within two weeks.

Ask your dentist what kind of materials are being used for fillings, crowns, and implants. Ask if there are other materials available besides mercury, and what is the least toxic. Find out if your dental plan, if you have one, will cover less toxic forms of material. Consider replacing old fillings, crowns, and so on, with less toxic material.

Here are some hints about how to make your trip to the dentist a more pleasant experience:

- If going to a new dentist, spell out your dental history, including your fears. A good dentist, and one you want to continue seeing, will listen and understand, and will go out of his or her way to make the experience easier for you. Keep in mind that few dentists actually enjoy the process themselves when it's their turn to sit in that chair.

- Remember, as with your total health care, you are in charge. Before any dental procedure, be sure you understand what will be done and why. Establish some ground rules, such as holding up your hand when you need the doctor to stop or asking the doctor to let you know before a shot is about to be given. If you are more comfortable with a mild sedative before the doctor begins working, ask if this is available. Be sure to have someone else drive you home afterward.[26]

- Try to relax. Don't drink coffee before the appointment, as this may increase your anxiety. Eat protein, not foods high in sugar, because protein has a calming effect. You might also try listening to relaxing music in advance of the procedure, then letting the music play in your mind while the doctor is working.[27]

Managing your medical care

It is up to you to know and understand your own health conditions, as well as your family health history. Become a consumer of health-care information. Ask questions, read health-care journals and magazines, and search the Internet to find information on specific diseases and treatment options.

Know your rights as a patient with regards to confidentiality, privacy, and security. You have a right to full information about the outcomes of care, treatment, and services so you can make the best decisions. You have the right to refuse treatment, as well as the right to seek a second opinion. Gone are the days when the family doctor made all the decisions for the patient, sometimes without bothering to explain what was happening. The patient is the consumer; the doctor is the provider of care. Your best option for quality care is to form a partnership with your health-care providers, whose goals are the same as yours—your health. Try to develop with your doctor a good relationship in which you share information openly and work together toward the goal of restoring your health.

To enhance two-way communication with your doctor, keep the following four principles in mind when you go visit him or her:

Identify your main concern before you go. The first thing your doctor will want to know is your "chief complaint"—what worries you the most. Ask yourself: *If my doctor could only do one thing for me, what would I ask for?* To ensure that you are clear about this, list all your health concerns, prioritize them, and then limit your list to three to five items. Note when you first noticed each of these problems, how they began, what the symptoms are, how often they occur, what brings them on, and what seems to make them better or worse. Be prepared to describe any treatment you have already had for each problem. Bring information on any prescriptions you may be taking— bring the bottles themselves, if possible, including over-the-counter preparations you are using.

Speak up. In order to help you, doctors need to understand your situation. Your notes will help you be clear, concise, and complete, while also conveying your fears and concerns. The doctor will ask questions, which you should answer as completely and accurately as possible. Otherwise, the doctor can't plan the best treatment for any conditions you may have. It is in your best interest to divulge even the most sensitive information. Cooperation will enhance your ability to take charge of your health easier in the long run, because it makes you part of a health-care team in which all the "players" are acting in agreement.

Ask questions. Your doctor will perform a physical examination to confirm the suspected diagnosis. Laboratory and other tests will assist in this process. When the doctor explains the diagnosis, repeat back what you think you have heard. For example, you might say, "If I understand correctly, you are saying..." Ask questions to better grasp the diagnosis and treatment plan, such as: "When should I expect to see improvement?" or "What are the signs that should tell me to come back to see you?" If you forget to ask something, write it down for next time or call the doctor's office. Be pleasantly persistent until you get the answers that you need.

If there are issues you want to discuss and the doctor doesn't mention them, raise them yourself. Don't be afraid to bring up sensitive topics or issues. Ask about the effects of diet and weight loss, exercise, stress, sleep, use of nonprescription drugs, tobacco, alcohol, or sexual practices. Inquire about the risks or benefits of alternative treatments you may be considering. Ask if a second opinion would be helpful.

Tell the doctor when you don't understand. If you get confused or the doctor is talking "over your head," then say, "I don't understand." If you still don't understand, even when further explanations have been given, ask for audio or written resources that you can study. Use the Internet to fill in any gaps. A big part of managing your medical problems is your knowledge of and participation in the treatment process.

Managing your medications

Your physician or dentist may prescribe a medication or medications to treat your illness or alleviate your pain. It is important to know your medications and what they are used for, as well as any common side effects and possible interactions with anything else you may be taking, either prescription or over-the-counter medications, as well as any vitamins, minerals, or herbs. Keep these things in mind:

- Know your medical conditions by name. If possible, carry the information on a 3 x 5 index card. Include the names and numbers of your emergency contacts, your doctor(s), and which medications you are taking and why. Record the medication and dosage. Keep this card where you can find it when needed.[28]

- Be consistent. When filling prescriptions, use the same pharmacist so that he or she becomes familiar enough with your medical condition and medications to alert you to any possible drug interactions.[29]

- Clean out your medicine cabinet regularly—at least once a year—of both prescription and over-the-counter medications. Throw away unused medications. Store medications in their original containers or boxes so that you have the name and dosage available when needed.[30]

- Read and become familiar with common side effects of any medications you are taking. Serious drug side effects can cause hospitalization or even death. People at risk of more serious drug side effects are those who are taking a lot of medications, have had their medications changed recently, have more than one doctor prescribing medications, have literacy or language difficulties, or have confusion or dementia, which makes them unable to remember taking their medications.

- For those who have memory loss, a specially designed box that organizes a week's worth of pills is a good idea. Noncompliance with medications is an issue for the elderly or for anyone with memory problems, which can result in either over- or under-medicating.

Talk to your health-care professional about the medications prescribed to you. Ask questions about what to do if you miss a dose and if there is anything you should avoid when taking the medication, such as driving or being in the sun.

Managing chronic illness

Despite everything you do, you or someone you love may develop a chronic illness. For most people, coming to grips with this reality is a very difficult and long process. One of our good friends, endocrinologist Dr. Curtis Harris, described this process, which he has seen in many of his patients with diabetes:

> When I first tell a patient that he has diabetes, he wants to know everything possible about it—how to treat it, especially how to treat it without medication. He avoids the word *diabetes* and uses phrases like "my sugar is high" to describe it. He'll start exercising and lose weight, research and often purchase and use alternative treatments he finds available on the Internet. In other words, he'll do everything possible to avoid what he sees as the stigma of being a diabetic, as if he can somehow turn back the clock.
>
> This process can continue a year or more, but then he gradually returns to his old lifestyle, and the weight and symptoms return, sometimes worse than before if he passes a point of resignation where he believes that he simply cannot help himself. At this point, he may become critical of the medical establishment, including me as its representative, because he thinks it was up to us to fix him and we failed. Often he will end up seeking treatment somewhere else—usually from a specialist or a practitioner of alternative medicine, or both.
>
> The only patients who actually do well are those who accept or "own" their disease, as an alcoholic must do by saying, at AA meetings, "I'm Joe, and I'm an alcoholic." In other words, in order to do well, a diabetic patient must acknowledge that diabetes is

not just out there as an enemy, but that diabetes is now part of his identity, like his gender or the color of his eyes or skin.

On one level, this may seem like giving up, because no one wants to have diabetes or any other chronic illness. But here's where faith can turn this on its head, for the Scriptures tell us that we're all part of a creation that is permeated by sin and "groaning" due to the apparent futility of the struggle to survive. From time to time this futility taps us on the shoulder, slaps us in the face, or worse. Those who gain most from such experiences realize that they really are dust, and to dust they are returning. For some believers, part of being "dust" is having diabetes or some other chronic disease, and along with it an opportunity to learn and grow and change. In other words, the route to taking charge of chronic illness is to give it to the One who is in charge of the entire universe, asking Him to somehow use the whole experience to further His purpose for your life.

The following are suggestions to keep in mind as you seek to practice preventative health care or when you become ill:

AN OUNCE OF PREVENTION

1. Make and keep regular medical and dental checkups. Use a date you'll remember as a reminder—for example, on New Year's Day, celebrate another year of good health by making a note to call your doctors' offices tomorrow.

2. Stay informed and up-to-date regarding products and practices that enhance health.

3. Practice the healthful habits you've learned about in this book, and avoid anything that might threaten your health.

4. Monitor your own weight and blood pressure; perform self-examinations regularly.

5. Make your home safe from pollution, toxins, allergens, and infectious bacteria.

6. Take responsibility for your own health and the health of those you care about.

A POUND OF CURE

1. Take care of any developing dental issues as soon as possible.

2. Be aware of your insurance coverage and limits.

3. Know your rights and responsibilities as a patient.

4. Make yourself part of your own treatment team.

5. Know the medications you're taking, and why; know their possible side effects and interactions with other prescription or over-the-counter medications or supplements you are using.

6. Take charge of chronic illness by learning all you can about its management, while gaining all you can from the experience.

My Priorities

List your top three priorities in your plan for practicing prevention:

1. _____

2. _____

3. _____

List your top three priorities in your plan for treating your current conditions or illnesses:

1. _____

2. _____

3. _____

Chapter 7

Nurture and Protect Your Relationships

*Learning the Value of Connection
With Friends and Family*

It is not good that the man should be alone.

—GENESIS 2:18, KJV

To be in a relationship with someone is one of the greatest gifts we are given in this world, and our relationships with other people are often key ingredients in our ability to live happier, healthier lives.

Good relationships are good for you—physically, psychologically, socially, and spiritually. "There's a good deal of research showing that people who have strong, enduring social support have better health outcomes," said Frank Baker, PhD, vice president for behavioral research at the national office of the American Cancer Society in Atlanta. "Friends and relatives are important because they help you deal with the adversities of life; you're likely to have better health and be happier."[1]

Emotional support from family and friends buffers stressful life events and reduces the risk of (and speeds recovery from) depression.[2] When you've had a bad day, it always helps to have a friend to call for a heart-to-heart talk or just to take you out to do something fun or silly. People with these kinds of strong relationships—including marriage, other family members, and friends—live longer.[3] In fact, they may even be more resistant to infection due to better immune system functioning.[4] Social support is also associated with less cigarette smoking, less alcohol abuse, a healthier diet, more exercise, and better sleep quality.[5]

Social support also helps people recover from illness. Research on people with cardiovascular diseases suggests that close relationships help protect heart attack survivors against future cardiovascular problems. British researcher Dr. Francis Creed and his colleagues focused on 583 men and women, all about age sixty, all hospitalized with heart attacks. Each patient was asked about emotional issues, including what social support they had. The patients also took tests to determine whether they were anxious or depressed. A year later, those who had a close personal confidant had 50 percent less risk of dying from heart disease than those without a close confidant. In describing his findings, Dr. Creed explained, "It's the degree of intimacy of close relationships—not the number of social contacts—that appears to protect heart health." A close confidant, he said, is "usually a spouse or partner, but not necessarily. It may be a very, very close friend or relative."[6]

Social support from friends, family members, and even pets can help people with cancer and other illnesses live longer. According to Denise Mann, who reported on recent research in a WebMD Medical News article:

> One study found that women with breast cancer lived longer over a seven-year period and had less chance of relapse if their social support network was large and strong. Karen Weihs, MD, of the George Washington University Medical Center in Washington DC, came to this conclusion after studying ninety women newly diagnosed with breast cancer. Among the women she studied, those who listed nine supportive people they could call on for help were just 60 percent as likely to die or have a cancer recurrence than the women who listed six or fewer people in their support network.[7]

By contrast, the Victorian Population Health Survey of 2001 conducted in and around the area of Melbourne, Australia, found that:

> People with few social networks were more likely to report fair to poor health and to be experiencing some level of psychological distress. They were also less likely to feel valued by society....Mental distress as a result of social isolation and lack of social support has been shown to increase the likelihood of heart disease, complications in pregnancy and delivery, and suicide.[8]

Let's face it: you were created to be in relationship with other people, and the more you "connect" with others, the happier and healthier you will be.

MARRIAGE IS HEALTH ENHANCING

There are hundreds of studies that support the idea that marriage is good for your health. The excellent online resource Teen Care Center affirms that marriage is a primary source of social support for many adults. In numerous surveys married individuals report greater happiness and life satisfaction and have a lower risk of depression than their unmarried counterparts.[9]

In the article "Why Marriage Is Good for You," Maggie Gallagher gives evidence to support the benefits of a healthy marital relationship.[10]

- *"Marriage lowers the risk* that both men and women will become victims of violence....A 1994 Justice Department report...found that single and divorced women were four to five times more likely to be victims of violence than wives; bachelors were four times more likely to be violent-crime victims than husbands."

- *"Marriage is good for your mental health.* Married men and women are less depressed, less anxious, and less psychologically distressed than single, divorced, or widowed Americans. By contrast, getting divorced lowers both men's and women's mental health, increasing depression and hostility, and lowering one's self-esteem and a sense of personal mastery and purpose in life."

- *Your children will be better off.* Research shows "...that children reared outside of intact marriages are much more likely than other kids to slip into poverty, become victims of child abuse, fail at school and drop out, use illegal drugs, launch into premature sexual activity, become unwed teen mothers, divorce, commit suicide and experience other signs of mental illness, become physically ill, and commit crimes and go to jail. On average, children reared outside of marriage are less successful in their careers...."

Because marriage is a partnership in every area, it is more than just an economic or business arrangement. It is a combining of shared values and shared lives—and it leads to a greater sense of meaning and purpose than can be found in most other relationships. A partner throughout life—somebody who is "on your side" through thick and thin—does wonders for helping people to live happier, healthier lives.

A HEALTHY HOME AND FAMILY LIFE

Along those lines, a healthy marriage is the foundation of a healthy family. "The family has the function of nurturing human beings in relationships that are rich with creative possibilities. It provides the surroundings in which persons enhance rather than exploit one another, in which mistakes may be made and forgiveness realized. The family [is the primary relational context in which parents and children] have a sense of intimacy and belonging. [The family] is intended by God to be that basic community in which personhood is fostered. The family should not become centered on itself, but should be seen as a base from which its members move out to participate in society."[11]

Healthy families are comprised of individuals who set aside, plan, and enjoy time, recreation, and other activities together. They are committed to each other's welfare and happiness. They often create and celebrate traditions unique to their family, which connect them with their family roots. Within the family unit, members work and play together in the context of mutual commitment and respect, while allowing freedom for self-expression. The members of the family know that they can depend on each other in good times and times of adversity.[12]

Healthy families value and include members of the extended family, such as grandparents and other relatives, in their activities and plans. They provide a context in which values, skills, and behaviors are learned by example, observation, and experience. They nurture loyalty and trust between the members, who often express encouragement and appreciation for each other. They provide a safe place to express love, honesty, understanding, patience, and forgiveness and to learn skills related to communication and conflict resolution. Parents are not dictators, and children have a voice in decision making and in enforcing the rules. The group, as a unit, has a sense of purpose in its life together and a commitment to a greater good than its own happiness.[13]

HONORING YOUR PARENTS

In her article "Supportive Parents Promote Good Health," Jennifer Warner sets forth new scientific research that seems to indicate that the benefits of good parenting last long past childhood and well into a person's adult life. It has been known for some time that children who receive high levels of support from their parents during their formative years report fewer psychological and physical problems at that time. But research now suggests that those healthy effects will, in fact, persist throughout adulthood. Citing the March 2004 issue of the journal *Psychology and Aging*, Warner said:

Researchers found that the adults' current mental and physical health was strongly influenced not only by current levels of emotional support, but also by parental support they received in childhood. Specifically, a lack of parental support in childhood was linked to increased levels of depressive symptoms and chronic health conditions, such as high blood pressure, arthritis, and urinary problems in adulthood. The link appeared to be stronger for mental health problems than physical ones, but researchers say that may be due to differences in how chronic health conditions develop over time.[14]

A good relationship with your parents will benefit you throughout your entire lifetime. Here are some suggestions to continue to "honor" them, even as you—and they—grow older.[15]

- Remember that your parents gave you the gift of life, and be sure to thank them for it as often as you can. Your gratefulness for all the things they have done for you throughout the years should make you want to give back to them.

- Instead of blaming your parents for their shortcomings, focus on the positive things they have given you—the significant contributions that they may have made to your life. Of course, we all make mistakes, and your parents are human, just as you are. But when you choose to honor them more for who they are than the things that they may—or may not—have done, your relationship will become even richer and more rewarding in the long run.

- When you disagree with your parents, take care not to speak to them in a demeaning way—contradicting, correcting, or shaming them. Harsh talk has no place between children and parents.

- Support them as they age. This caring is implied in the apostle Paul's statement, "If anyone does not provide for his relatives, and especially for his immediate family, he has denied the faith and is worse than an unbeliever" (1 Tim. 5:8).

THE VALUE OF FRIENDSHIP

What does the word *friend* bring to your mind? Someone specific? A shared joke? Happy memories of good times together? Proverbs 18:24 says, "A man of many companions may come to ruin, but there is a friend who sticks closer than a brother."

Our friends are often our closest or most intimate confidants—those people to whom we can entrust our deepest secrets. It is possible to be friends with your relatives by blood or marriage, though your closest friends may be outside your family circle.

One mark of mental health is to have at least one close or intimate friend.[16] God was right when He said that it is not good for humans to be alone. Having such a friend could even save your life. In one study of persons who had been diagnosed with coronary artery disease, unmarried people who lacked a confidant were 50 percent less likely to survive during a five-year period than those with a confidant.[17]

Of all the biblical examples of friendship, the story of David and Jonathan (1 Samuel 19–20) is perhaps the most moving due to the interpersonal dynamics involved. David, the shepherd boy who had killed nine-foot-tall Goliath with his sling, would play his harp (which was like a modern guitar) for King Saul, Jonathan's father, to calm Saul when he was troubled. Over time, David and Jonathan became best friends. Jonathan bestowed on David very special gifts, and they kept each other's secrets. But when Saul became bent on killing David, the two young friends parted in tears and with an oath that they would always be friends. Later, after the deaths of Saul and Jonathan, David (who had become king) took Jonathan's lame son into the palace, as his own.

A genuine close or intimate friendship:

- Involves affectionate companionship.

- Often shares interests, pursuits, and passionate commitment to a cause.

- Involves a shared sense of caring and concern, a desire to see mutual growth and development, and a hope that the friend succeeds in life.

- Often involves doing something for the other, expecting nothing in return.

- Often involves sharing private thoughts and feelings without fear of judgment or critique, confident that the other will keep what is shared confidential.

- Takes time—learning about each other, making memories, helping each other grow.

- Includes encouragement, grace, and forgiveness.

- Involves trust, accountability, faithfulness, dependability, loyalty, and the acceptance of unconditional love.

- Often includes a commitment to the other's interests, even after death.[18]

Friends are burden bearers, secret keepers, fun sharers, and emotional supporters. Friends weep with you and rejoice with you. They are there during crisis or temptation. Friends counter isolation and loneliness. Like no other kind of relationships, friendships make life bearable and doable.

Having a friend keeps us sane, makes us laugh, and allows us to be who we really are. I (Dave) have a sign I hang on my tent in the Rockies during elk season: "Here I am my real self." I want my friends to know that whoever shares that camp with me can relax and be real, too.

To have friends, you must be a friend. True friendship involves reciprocity, give and take, without either party keeping score. True friendship involves transparency and vulnerability, which develop over time as trust is established. Most of the time most people hide behind masks out of fear of what others will think of them—except when they're with a true friend.

Being transparent and vulnerable is scary and risky because it leaves us open to hurt, possible criticism, rejection, and even betrayal since another human being knows our secrets. But in light of the physical, emotional, sociological, and spiritual benefits that come from having a friend and being a friend, the risk is worth taking.

For Christians, transparency with a trusting God is the foundation for interpersonal transparency. When we have learned to be open and trusting with God, whom we cannot see, it becomes easier to have these qualities in a relationship with a person we've come to know and trust.

FORGIVENESS AND RECONCILIATION

Sometimes friendships have "bumps in the road"—just like any other relationship. At those times, it's important to smooth out the bumps with one of the most precious gifts we can give a friend: the gift of forgiveness.

When you choose to forgive, what you are really doing is giving up the right to get even with the person who hurt you. When you truly forgive, you release *yourself* from the emotional prison of your resentment toward your friend.[19]

Forgiving other people replaces negative emotions with positive ones, which helps reduce stress. This, in turn, helps to reduce heart problems and other chronic illnesses. In an article in *Ladies Home Journal,* Nina Elder wrote: "Researchers now believe that letting go of grudges may fortify the heart and the immune system. 'When you're stuck in a grudge, you're isolated in your own suffering,' says Fred Luskin, PhD, author of *Forgive for Good* and director of the Stanford

Forgiveness Project. 'The long-term damage to the cardiovascular system from bitterness and resentment is clearly established.'"[20]

An article on PreventDisease.com states:

> Studies presented by [Charlotte C.] VanOyen-Witoliet [PhD] showed those who could forgive had reduced blood pressure and fewer heart problems. Those unable to forgive, regardless of whether the incident had occurred a long time ago, the offender had apologized, or even if the incident had not been very severe, showed higher blood-pressure rates, tension around the eyes, an increase in sweaty skin and overall higher stress levels. VanOyen-Witoliet also pointed out research suggesting hostile behavior is associated with heart disease and premature death. Those who forgave their offenders showed lower levels of hostility. Forgiveness, she says, "may buffer and ultimately enhance health."
>
> Michael E. McCullough of the National Institutes of Health…found similar findings when trying to measure forgiveness. Those who forgive, he says, are replacing old, negative feelings, with new, positive feelings. "Forgiveness becomes a contrast between before and after," McCullough says. "The more you say you still want to get even, the less you are forgiving."[21]

Benefits of forgiveness such as those listed here might motivate anyone to lay down their grudges and get on with life. For believers, however, there are much stronger motives, primary among them being to practice kindness and compassion because we have received these freely from God as a result of our faith in Christ. "Be kind and compassionate to one another," the apostle Paul wrote, "forgiving each other, just as in Christ God forgave you" (Eph. 4:32). The scriptural view is that we all, like sheep, have gone astray, and therefore we stand equally in need of forgiveness. No one is good, except God, though this is very hard to believe about ourselves, especially when far more evil people abound in our world or when some hurtful or even hateful thing has been done to us. In the Lord's Prayer and other places in Scripture, Jesus made it clear that our own sense of having been forgiven impels us, even compels us, to forgive others, for whatever reason, from our hearts.

Jesus Himself demonstrated this kind of forgiveness in relation to His own friends, the disciples, all of whom forsook Him and fled when He needed them most. One of the more poignant accounts in the New Testament involves Jesus and Peter, one of the Lord's most intimate friends and who denied Him three times on the night Jesus was taken into custody. Later, Jesus seeks out Peter and, in the presence of the some of the other disciples, the Lord lets the fisherman know that he is forgiven by mirroring his denials with three questions that renewed Peter's calling.[22]

The Lord's calling to believers today is to become as much like Him as possible, which includes forgiving others as we have been forgiven, so we can live fully in the present (not enslaved to the past) with an eye toward the future. This kind of grace extended toward others can be a powerful witness to a world driven by hatred and revenge that His way is better.

Here are some suggestions for practicing forgiveness in your relationships, even with people who may have hurt you deeply:

- Acknowledge the facts and the depths of the hurt you feel.

- Acknowledge the resentment, bitterness, even hatred, and give them to the Lord, along with the right to get even.

- Separate the person from the act that has hurt you.

- Take responsibility for any part you played in what happened.

- Talk to the person who hurt you, in person or in a letter. Be honest—pretending will not change anything. Note: If that person is deceased, write the letter, then burn it as an offering to the Lord.

- Reconcile with the person, if possible.

- If the person refuses to acknowledge they did anything wrong, leave the rest to God, who will take care of it far better than you can. (See Romans 12:19.)

Friendship is one of the best gifts God has given to us. Here are some further suggestions to help you maintain great relationships and lead a happier, healthier life.

- Look for and affirm positives in others; try to make most of your interactions positive.

- Laugh together. Refuse to take yourself, or what's happening, too seriously.

- Keep your perspective. Learn not to sweat the small stuff.

- Realize that how you handle conflict, which every relationship has, will be the key to how long the relationship in question lasts.

- If you have an argument, listen more than you speak. Focus on actions, not motives. Keep things in the present. Never say "never," or "always," or "you're just like your mother (or father)."

- Have a "Plan B" for most things. Don't be an "insister"— one who has to have it your way or no way. Be adaptable and flexible.

- If you experience frustration, walk it off. Getting in somebody's face until you win will damage your relationship.

- Take a break or change your setting. An outing or an overnight away can help you see things differently.

- When you're wrong, admit it. When you're right, don't say, "I told you so."

- If you hurt someone, apologize, ask forgiveness, and make amends if possible.

- Love people and use things—never the reverse.

- Keep short accounts. Even little unresolved hurts can build a wall over time.

So, what's your plan? Write it here.

My Plan

Three things I will do today to foster great relationships with other people.

1. _____

2. _____

3. _____

Three things I will try to do within the next three months to keep up my relationships with these family members and friends.

1. _____

2. _____

3. _____

SIMPLE HEALTH

Three things I will try to do within the next six months to continue to nurture my happy, healthy relationships.

1. _____

2. _____

3. _____

Today's date: _____ / _____ / _____

Chapter 8

Don't Worry, Be Happy

The Health Benefits of Keeping an Optimistic Outlook

> Eat your food with gladness, and drink your wine
> with a joyful heart, for it is now that God favors what
> you do....Enjoy life with your [spouse], whom you
> love....Whatever your hand finds to do, do it with
> all your might, for in the grave, where you are going,
> there is neither working nor planning nor knowledge
> nor wisdom.
>
> —ECCLESIASTES 9:7–10

"The pursuit of happiness." This phrase is embedded in our American heritage and is arguably an important part of the most stirring passage in the American Declaration of Independence: "We hold these truths to be self-evident, that all men are created equal, that they are endowed by their Creator with certain unalienable rights, that among these are life, liberty, and the pursuit of happiness."

For all the talk about happiness, it's actually difficult to define. What exactly is happiness anyway? Hundreds of years ago, Aristotle put it this way: "Happiness is the meaning and the purpose of life, the whole aim and end of human existence."

In recent years the study of happiness and what hinders or contributes to it has become more scientific. In "The New Science of Happiness," Claudia Wallis describes the rapid development of "positive psychology."[1] The movement's leader, Martin E. P. Seligman, PhD, author of the book *Authentic Happiness*, states on his Web site:

> Most Americans equate "happiness" with a cheery emotion, a Goldie Hawn smile, and boundless optimism...[though] many thoughtful people throughout the world view our have-a-nice-day mentality as empty-headed and heedless. Positive Psychology is intended as a serious and universal approach to understanding and building emotional well being, and it is decidedly not focused on shallow, self-indulgent pleasures.[2]

As earnestly desired and pursued as happiness is, it is a difficult concept to explain. For example, if you were to ask some passersby to define happiness, you would most likely hear phrases such as "to experience pleasure," "to have good fortune," "to feel glad," "to delight in or enjoy something," or even "to feel blessed." The latter is a phrase most often connected with faith, in which one's happiness is a more settled version known as joy and linked to a sense of gratitude for having received God's love.

Before we try to describe happiness and its health benefits, let's pause for a moment so you can estimate your own current level of happiness. The following quiz is based on ideas about happiness from a variety of sources, and it should give you a good idea of how happy you are—right now. (After you're finished with this chapter, you may wish to return to this quiz and complete it again for comparison.)

TAKE THE HAPPINESS QUIZ

DIRECTIONS: Enter a number between 0 and 4 for every statement below that indicates how true the statement is for you. Before you complete the quiz, estimate your current happiness quotient (your current overall level of happiness) on a scale from 0 to 100. Then compare your estimate to the total after you answer the questions and add up your score. The total is your "happiness quotient"—the level of your current happiness as a percentage of the maximum possible:

0   *Never true*
1   *Sometimes true*
2   *Undecided/Neutral*
3   *Usually true*
4   *Always true*

1. I enjoy simple things that often don't cost anything. _____

2. I tend to bounce back well from adversity. _____

3. I don't worry about the future. _____

4. I set realistic goals and am gratified when I achieve them. _____

5. I ometimes get so involved with work or hobbies that I lose all sense of time passing. _____

6. I wake up most mornings with a positive attitude toward the day ahead. _____

7. I try to gain from constructive criticism. _____

8. I enjoy pleasurable activities but am not addicted to any of them. _____

9. More money, things, power, or prestige would not make me happier. _____

10. I approach life's challenges optimistically. _____

11. I am grateful for what I have, without comparing myself to others. _____

12. I do not experience boredom. _____

13. I derive a sense of satisfaction from my work. _____

14. I do not dwell on things from the past that cannot be changed. _____

15. I don't spend money or buy things in order to feel happier. _____

16. I feel a sense of gratitude to God for His blessings. _____

17. I believe that joy is possible even in the midst of great difficulty. _____

18. I am not driven to achieve approval or recognition of my efforts. _____

19. I am not weighed down or distracted by financial concerns. _____

20. My greatest joy comes from glorifying God and enjoying my relationship with Him. _____

21. I am able to celebrate the achievements of others, without envy or jealousy. _____

22. I believe that my being here has made a positive difference in the world. _____

23. My times of greatest happiness have been shared with friends or family. _____

24. I try to build on my strengths instead of focusing on my weaknesses. _____

25. My sense of self-worth is linked to knowing that God values me. _____

Total: My happiness quotient today is (add up 1–25): _____

Date: _____ / _____ / _____

TRUE HAPPINESS INVOLVES THE WHOLE PERSON

Our belief is that health-enhancing happiness involves and affects every arena of life—biological, psychological, sociological, and spiritual. While happy *feelings* may be pleasurable for a while, such feelings inevitably diminish when the circumstances that produced them change. In other words, the "happiness" that so many people long for is like a butterfly they may glimpse from time to time as they chase it frenetically across the field called life. Many never catch it, and those who do often discover that pursuing happiness was more pleasurable than its capture.

By contrast, true happiness—the kind that makes a long-term difference in our lives—is not an emotion we feel as a result of something that happens outside of ourselves. Instead, as Webster's dictionary defines, *happiness* is "a state of well-being and contentment." For people of faith, happiness is directly related to experiencing the grace of God in its variety of expressions. Such people have learned that the secret of happiness is not in its pursuit, but in allowing a transcendent, supernatural joy to take up residence within them, joining its cousins contentment, serenity, and gratitude. We'll return to these when we consider the spiritual components of happiness.

HAPPINESS HAS PHYSICAL BENEFITS

Common sense tells us that happiness is healthful. Now science is catching up. We're headed into a few pages of scientific stuff, but don't let your eyes glaze over. We just want you to know that a number of studies have been completed, more are underway, and what's been ascertained thus far.

One group conducting research on multiple levels is the University of Wisconsin's Health Emotions Research Institute. Current projects include:

- Effects of Stress and Mood on Disease Progression and Mortality in Free-Ranging Monkeys
- The Biological Substrates of Resilience

- Effects of Social Contact on Modulating Responses to Negative Emotionally Provoking Events
- The Biological Bases of Positive Affective Styles, and The Biological Consequences of Meditation[3]

Gerontologist David J. Demko, PhD, online editor of AgeVenture Syndicated News Service, says:

There is now a vast body of research showing that people who often suffer negative emotions tend to die younger than people who face life with positive emotions. According to Dr. Susan S. Knox, National Institute of Health (NIH), negative emotions include "worrying incessantly, feeling friendless, and flying off the handle..." Knox studies the interaction of psychology and physiology at the NIH's National Heart, Lung, and Blood Institute. "Emotional factors have a major impact on physical health," Knox [told] *New Choices* magazine. "Negative emotions...often lead to weaker immune systems, higher rates of heart disease, and other major health problems."

If negative emotions tend to shorten one's life, then do positive emotions tend to lengthen life? Good question. The answer is a yes. Researchers at the University of Wisconsin-Madison have found that people with long histories of positive relationships tend to have lower levels of stress hormones....[4]

Rich Bayer, PhD, claims that:

In a broad-based study of adults aged 65 and older, it was shown that positive emotion was a strong predictor of how long people lived. Happy people in the study were half as likely to die and half as likely to become disabled as compared to people who were generally sad. There's another fascinating and perhaps unusual scientific finding. Those who live happy lives have a greater tolerance for physical pain than those who are sad.[5]

In the *Time* magazine article "The Biology of Joy," Michael D. Lemonick reported:

As researchers have gained an understanding of the physical characteristics of a happy brain, they have come to see that those traits
have a powerful influence on the rest of the body. People who rate
in the upper reaches of happiness on psychological tests develop
about 50 percent more antibodies than average in response to flu
vaccines....

Others have discovered that happiness or related mental states
like hopefulness, optimism, and contentment appear to reduce
the risk or limit the severity of cardiovascular disease, pulmonary disease, diabetes, hypertension, colds, and upper-respiratory
infections as well.... According to a Dutch study of elderly patients
published in November 2004, those upbeat mental states reduced
an individual's risk of death 50 percent over the study's nine-year
duration.[6]

Though research is just starting to explore the scientific frontiers
related to the biological effects of happiness, it is clear that a healthy
dose of happiness is good for you! This is as true today as it was three
thousand years ago when Solomon wrote: "A cheerful look brings joy
to the heart, and good news gives health to the bones" (Prov. 15:30),
and "A cheerful heart is good medicine" (Prov. 17:22).

POSITIVE ATTITUDES ENHANCE HAPPINESS

Our list of suggestions at the end of the chapter includes a variety
of attitudes that affect happiness. So here we will limit our focus to
the following psychological contributors to happiness—optimism,
resilience, and satisfaction.

Optimism

Perhaps you've heard the story about the optimist and pessimist
who went duck hunting with the constant companion of the optimist,
a Labrador retriever. When the first duck was bagged, the dog's master said to his friend, "Watch this." To the dog he said, "Fetch." The
dog jumped overboard, walked across the water, retrieved the duck,
stepped into the boat, and laid the bird at the feet of his master. The

pessimist made no comment. When the second duck was downed, the dog repeated the amazing feat; still no comment from the pessimist. The third time, however, the pessimist could no longer contain his enthusiasm. "Can't swim, can he?" he said.

According to Webster's dictionary, *optimism* is "an inclination to put the most favorable construction upon actions and events or to anticipate the best possible outcome." An optimist thinks that a half-full glass of water is in the process of being filled, but a pessimist sees it as half-empty on its way to being completely drained. The difference is not in reality—the glass is both half-full and half-empty; the difference is in the interpretation one puts on what one sees.

Although reality is ultimately the same for optimists and pessimists—life will always have its ups and downs—optimists enjoy the journey so much more, and they are likely to be happier, healthier, and live longer, more enjoyable lives as well!

Laura Kubzansky, PhD, a health psychologist at Harvard's School of Public Health, tracked 1,300 men for ten years and found that heart disease among optimistic men was half the rate for men who weren't optimistic. "It was a much bigger effect than we expected," she said. "We also looked at pulmonary function, since poor pulmonary function is predictive of a whole range of bad outcomes, including premature mortality, cardiovascular disease and chronic obstructive pulmonary disease." Optimists were much healthier. "I'm an optimist," she says, "but I didn't expect results like this."[7]

The bottom line is that optimism contributes to happiness and happiness is health-enhancing, so the next time you see a glass of water, try to view it with realistic optimism. You'll be happier for it.

Resilience

The ability to "bounce back" from tough times is a key element in happiness.

There are a number of good books available on the subject of resilience, among the best being *Resilience* by Christian psychiatrist Frederic Flach. Flach noted that the healthiest among his patients were not those who were "strong" in the face of adversity but those who had been broken by adversity only to experience a remarkable reintegration and renewal of their lives.

> I began to look at many of my patients as being among the healthiest people I knew. Many of them had appropriately collapsed in the face of significant stress and change. What on the surface may have looked like a failure to cope was, in fact, evidence of resilience. The temporary state of confusion and emotional anguish in which they found themselves represented a singular opportunity to resolve old wounds, discover new ways to deal with life, and effectively reorganize themselves.[8]

In Flach's opinion, "The most vital ingredient of resilience is faith."[9] When we place our trust and hope in the Lord, He restores our lives—and a deep and abiding joy will be the inevitable result.

Satisfaction

While satisfaction also contributes to happiness, for many people it remains elusive. The Rolling Stones released the number-one hit "(I Can't Get No) Satisfaction" in May 1965, but the song, which stayed on the charts for fourteen weeks, is still popular today. Why? Because it captures in just a few words how many people feel about being told by Madison Avenue that they need newer, more, or different things or experiences in order to be happy. The song's popularity continues perhaps because, in a broader sense, it expresses the endless inner tension of unmet dreams and unfulfilled expectations in an era when many think that what they have is not quite enough or good enough, whether it be notoriety, money, sex, power, or possessions.

How much really is enough to make us happy? For many, the answer seems to be: "Just a little more than I have now." So they work longer hours to make more money or achieve things that cannot satisfy. In *The 100 Simple Secrets of Happy People*, David Niven, PhD, tells the story of "Arthur," an advertising executive who, on his way to the top worked six-day work weeks with long hours daily plus brought work home, woke up to reality in the hospital following triple-bypass heart surgery.

During three weeks of recovery, his family and best friends saw more of him than they had for decades. He cherished the time. Arthur's wife asked him if he really needed to work the schedule he had. Did they need more money? Did he really need another promotion? Arthur...realized he had more than he needed and that the opportunity to reconnect with his family was the greatest gift he could be given.[10]

For others, however, overall satisfaction with life—what we would call "true satisfaction"—is a more settled reality. It's usually not so much related to material wealth or possessions, but to simple things like gardening, involvement in sports and exercise, an enjoyable job, positive relationships, social activities, recreation and hobbies, and faith and faith-related activities.

Ultimately, the Scriptures make it clear that God Himself is the only true source of satisfaction:

> Satisfy us in the morning with your unfailing love, that we may sing for joy and be glad all our days.
>
> —PSALM 90:14

> Why spend money on what is not bread, and your labor on what does not satisfy? Listen, listen to me, and eat what is good, and your soul will delight in the richest of fare. Give ear and come to me; hear me, that your soul may live.
>
> —ISAIAH 55:2–3

SOCIOLOGICAL FACTORS INFLUENCING HAPPINESS

Happiness, for most people, is not just a private matter, but it occurs in a social context of some type. For example, work can occupy more than half our waking hours, day by day, year by year, until we either retire or expire. Sadly, many people work only because they must—to earn a living, support the family, and so forth—making "bricks for Pharaoh" without a great deal of satisfaction or gratification. These factors underlie a 2004 Gallup poll's finding that 70 percent of American workers are disengaged from their work, at an annual cost of nearly $300 billion in lost productivity. Fifty-four percent work on "autopilot" day-to-day, but most astonishingly, 17 percent were "actively disengaged"—actively undermining their co-workers' accomplishments. A follow-up release by the Gallup organization in January 2005 stated that 54 percent of actively disengaged workers believe that their work lives are having a negative effect on their physical health.[11]

Perhaps you can identify with this, even if you're not engaging in workplace sabotage. One person we know was so unhappy with her work situation that she developed symptoms related to anxiety. She disliked her work and the long daily commute, even though she performed with excellence that was regularly recognized. Her doctor, in the process of diagnosis and treatment, took the time to ask about her life situation, which included many pressures, the most negative of which was her work. "Have you considered finding other work?" the doctor asked, to which the patient could only respond, "I'd love to work elsewhere, but I would lose the benefits, and that would put my family at risk." A few months later, the patient and her husband decided to take the risk. They became a one-salary family while she took a short refresher course in nursing, which was her real love. She quickly found a new position with less pay and benefits, but a lot more satisfaction, because her new job was aligned with the direction of her calling, which was to help other people.

Of course, not everyone is in a situation where changing jobs is an option, though most workers will do so as many as seven times during their careers. When job change is not an option, attitude change is still possible. Even when your job is not very stimulating or rewarding, you can make it rewarding by embracing whatever you have to do as your vocation (calling). You can offer it up to God as an act of worship, as did Brother Lawrence, who for more than forty years washed pots and pans and repaired sandals as his gift to God and his fellow priests. His thoughts about the spirituality of work and many other matters were collected and published in the book *The Practice of the Presence of God*.[12]

Other social contexts can increase your happiness and thus enhance your health, including participating in group (community) endeavors such as hobbies, sports, clubs, or church activities.

There are as many kinds of groups as there are interests. So a good place to start is by taking an inventory of your interests, which may include recreational activities like softball or swimming, creative tasks like painting or needlepoint, or hobbies like stamp collecting or mushrooming. List everything that you really enjoy—from archery to ventriloquism, astronomy to zoology, cultivating apples to zucchini, and everything in between—and then try to find a group of people locally that is focused on whatever is your most passionate interest. Over time the kindred spirits you meet may become your closest personal friends.

You might even assemble a group of fun-loving friends and get together on a regular basis. Recently one group we know about went together for a lesson in belly dancing. What made this so unusual is that you would never picture these dignified mature women doing this. The one that teaches at a seminary went to the public library after the lesson and rented all their videos on belly dancing. Now the whole group is studying belly dancing. They've discovered that all females in Morocco belly dance. They're doing more research to find out why. The point is that small groups of like-minded people can result in a lot of fun doing things they might not otherwise imagine, laughing all the way.

SPIRITUAL COMPONENTS OF HAPPINESS

In his book *Finding Happiness in the Most Unlikely Places*, Donald W. McCullough thoroughly examines the Beatitudes of Jesus—eight simple, yet profound, sayings that turn typical human ideas about happiness on their heads. Happiness is not:

- Feeling satisfied with yourself—Jesus said the poor in spirit are blessed.

- Feeling cheerful—Jesus said that mourners are blessed.

- Having power over yourself or others—Jesus said the meek are blessed.

- Feeling fulfilled—Jesus said those who hunger and thirst for righteousness are blessed.

- Being detached from human suffering—Jesus said the merciful are blessed.

- Freedom to do many things—Jesus said the pure in heart are blessed.

- Escape from stress and tension—Jesus said the peace-makers are blessed.

- Being accepted by the world—Jesus said those who are persecuted are blessed.[13]

The Beatitudes are about more than *looking at life* from a different perspective; they are about *living life* within the context of a relationship with God through faith in Christ. This allows us to know Him, to cease our striving for significance, meaning, and happiness, and to rest in Him and His truth. As Augustine wrote: "This, therefore, is the complete satisfaction of souls, that is, the happy life: to know precisely and perfectly Him through whom you are led into the truth, the nature of the truth you enjoy, and the bond that connects you with the Supreme Measure!"

Knowing and doing God's will is the route to real happiness because it takes all the pressure off of us to take care of ourselves, to compete, to achieve, to do anything other than *be* His followers as we go through the process of learning and becoming more like Him. This process may take us through dark valleys we never imagined existed or to mountain peaks of exultation, but in the end it will not be the experiences that count, but the fact that in all of them He was there with us.

And this leads to a deep sense of joyful and grateful recognition that He, the master storyteller, has allowed our journeys to be part of the ultimate plot in which He uses people like us as part of His plan of redemption to bring beauty from ashes, good from evil. While we may not be able to see how what we're experiencing can possibly contribute to or even be a part of this plot, we can take heart and find joy in knowing that the story ends with the eradication of all pain and sadness and the renewal of all things. Revelation 21:3–4 says, "Now the dwelling of God is with men, and he will live with them. They will be his people, and God himself will be with them and be their God. He will wipe every tear from their eyes. There will be no more death or mourning or crying or pain, for the old order of things has passed away."

SUGGESTIONS FOR INCREASING YOUR HAPPINESS

1. *Be thankful.* Start a gratitude journal.[14] Each night, write at least one thing in it for which you want to thank God. Yes, we know that many secular advisors promote this concept. But pity the poor secularist who, when he or she feels gratitude, has no one to thank! Besides, an attitude of gratitude was really God's idea,[15] perhaps because He knew it would bring us greater joy. If you find your gratitude is focused on a person, make a point to write that person a letter expressing your thanksgiving; then go visit them, if possible, and read the letter to them. You'll see your happiness double.

2. *Nurture something.* Gardening increases happiness. To paraphrase an anonymous pundit: "To increase your happiness for a while, get married. To increase your happiness permanently, get a garden." There is something renewing that connects us with the eternal Creator whose work is ongoing in us and through us when we see something green and alive coming out of the brown earth from seeds we planted. It brings real enjoyment to see the blossoms come and then the fruit.

3. *Get a pet.* One 1990 study conducted by Judith Siegel at the University of California, Los Angeles, seemed to

suggest that people on Medicaid or Medicare who own a pet visit the doctor less often.[16] Pets reduce anxiety and stress, provide unconditional love and affirmation, and give you a good reason to get out and get some exercise— all things that contribute to health and happiness.[17]

4. *Don't try to force happiness on yourself or anyone else.* Popular Christian books as well as secular self-help materials promote the idea that happiness is a choice. While it is true that happiness may result from a series of choices related to the concerns we've mentioned in this chapter, especially the spiritual ones, it is not reasonable to think that you can "be happy" by willing it so. True happiness is an inside-out thing, like water gushing from an artesian well. The source is more important than the water itself. In the case of joy, the only reliable source is the Spirit of God. Your choice, therefore, is not to try to be happy, but to allow the Spirit of God to do His work in your heart.

5. *Give happiness away*, and you'll get it back with interest. Ralph Waldo Emerson once said: "Happiness is a perfume which you cannot pour on someone else without getting some on yourself." When you focus on making those people around you happy, you'll find that happiness will come right back to you—more than you ever expected.

6. *Consider your work.* Ask yourself, "If I won the lottery today, would I still go to the same job tomorrow?" If the answer is yes, keep that job, and be happy you have it! If no, then ask yourself the next question: "If I won the lottery today and could do anything I wanted for the rest of my life, what would I do?" Next, write down three to five steps you could take over the next three years to move yourself from the work you're in to work that will bring

you meaning and fulfillment because it is more aligned with your personal sense of mission or calling in life.

7. *Don't try to buy happiness.* Too many people go deeply into debt trying to acquire that one more thing that seems to promise satisfaction. Instead of satisfaction, the increased debt often adds significant stress. The saying "he who dies with the most toys wins" is absolutely untrue. Stuff is nothing. What's really true is you can't take it with you, and that when you're gone, the only thing of substance you will actually leave behind will be the positive relationships that you formed along the way.

8. *Pray.* Each night before you fall asleep, pray the "Serenity Prayer" or some version of it in your own words:

God, give us grace to accept with serenity
The things that cannot be changed,
Courage to change the things
Which should be changed,
And the wisdom to distinguish
The one from the other.

Living one day at a time,
Enjoying one moment at a time,
Accepting hardship as a pathway to peace,
Taking, as Jesus did,
This sinful world as it is,
Not as I would have it,
Trusting that You will make all things right,
If I surrender to Your will,
So that I may be reasonably happy in this life,
And supremely happy with You forever in the next.

Amen.

—REINHOLD NIEBUHR (1892–1971)

Now return to the Happiness Quiz near the start of this chapter. Take it again, and compare your two scores, with a view toward how the scores have changed, and why. List specific ideas or insights in this chapter that have helped you understand happiness as it relates to health and how you plan to implement these in your own life. Incorporate them into your plan of action below.

What's your plan? Record it here:

My Plan

In the next month, to increase my happiness, I will:

1. _____

2. _____

3. _____

In the next three months, to increase my happiness, I will:

1. _____

2. _____

3. _____

In the next year, to increase my happiness, I will:

1. _____

2. _____

3. _____

Chapter 9

Help Somebody Else
Fostering a Lifestyle of "Doing Unto Others"

No act of kindness, however small, is ever wasted.

—AESOP

I (Dave) will never forget how one night a friend and I were dining together in a restaurant. When we bowed our heads and prayed over the food, someone saw us, then paid our bill without our knowledge. What a shock to try to pay the waiter, only to hear: "Your bill's already covered, sir. Another patron took care of it."

Wow! There really are generous people in the world, after all. You never know when you will meet one, but they are out there, doing their "random acts of kindness" day after day. Since then, I've done a few such things myself—paid somebody's bill at the grocery store when they didn't have enough cash, for example, or leaving all the cash I was carrying at the time as a tip for the young waitress trying to raise her son alone. In terms of helping somebody else, what goes around comes around—and we don't mean financially. We mean it in overall wellness terms. When you help somebody—whether you've donated blood, money, time, or just helped someone across the street—you help yourself through an act of "unselfish regard for or devotion to the welfare of others" (known as *altruism*).

SIMPLE HEALTH

In his 1956 book *The Stress of Life*, Hans Selye encouraged what he called "altruistic egoism," not just for the effect such altruism might have on others, but also for what it does for the helper. It creates:

> …feelings of accomplishment and security in ourselves through the inspiration in others of love, good will and gratitude for what we have done or are likely to do in the future.[1]

Selye was a pioneer in studying the effects of stress on health. Adopting an altruistic lifestyle was one of his antidotes to what might otherwise negatively affect your health.

In February 1987, the magazine *Better Homes and Gardens* included an article about helping others. Readers were invited to describe how their own helping experiences made them feel. Of the 246 who responded:

- Sixty-eight percent said they experienced a distinct physical sensation while helping.

- Fifty percent described a "high" feeling.

- Forty-three percent felt greater strength and energy.

- Twenty-eight percent felt "warm."

- Twenty-two percent felt calmer and less depressed.

- Twenty-one percent experienced greater self-worth.

- Thirteen percent experienced fewer aches and pains.[2]

Following publication of the article that included the above data, researcher Allan Luks circulated a seventeen-question survey among volunteers serving in various U.S. organizations. Analysis of the 3,296 responses showed a strong connection between helping and health. "Helping contributes to the maintenance of good health, and it can diminish the effect of diseases and disorders both serious and minor, psychological and physical," Luks wrote.[3]

Most of the volunteers reported what Luks labeled a "helper's high"—a long-lasting euphoric sensation that would even return when the altruistic acts were recalled. Luks and his colleagues found that the health-enhancing effects of doing good included:

- A more optimistic outlook
- Increased energy
- Better perceived health
- Decreased feelings of loneliness and depression
- Better weight control
- Less pain
- A greater sense of relaxation and improvement in sleep
- A stronger immune system[4]

One of our colleagues, Sue, a marriage and family counselor, recalled how as a result of helping some clients achieve a breakthrough in their marriage, she experienced a helper's high that affected her in many ways:

> I had been feeling like I was getting nowhere with them and was wondering if I was really in the right profession and if I could help people gain insight and help into their problems. I had been praying that God would give me insight into their issues, and felt that He answered my prayer. Physically, I felt renewed, with more energy. Emotionally, I felt joy because there was a breakthrough.
>
> Relationally, I felt like I really connected with them, that we were all on the same page, and as a result our working relationship went to a new level. Spiritually, I felt reassured that God was there, guiding, giving direction, and it helped my faith. It was as if God was telling me to keep going, that I could make a difference in people's lives.

"TRY A LITTLE KINDNESS"

Acting with kindness involves choosing to treat someone you do not know as if he or she were your "kindred"—your brother or sister, mother or father. This is altruism at its best and practiced so remarkably by people like Father Damien, who ministered to the lepers of

Molokai, Hawaii, for fifteen years until he succumbed to the disease himself. Or Mother Teresa, who said, "Let no one ever come to you without leaving better and happier. Be the living expression of God's kindness: kindness in your face, kindness in your eyes, kindness in your smile." To the millions of poor and others in India and around the world who have benefited from the work of the Missionaries of Charity, which she founded in 1950, Mother Teresa was indeed a saint, as well as their kindred spirit.

Little by little, person by person, acts of kindness change the world even when done anonymously, impacting primarily the recipient and the one who acted kindly toward him or her. Sometimes kindness stories make the news, but more often they get posted on Web sites such as those maintained by HelpOthers.org or the Random Acts of Kindness Foundation.[5]

The following summary of health benefits related to kindness is adapted from the Web site of the Random Acts of Kindness Foundation:

> Helping contributes to the maintenance of good health, and it can diminish the effect of diseases and disorders, serious and minor, psychological and physical. Stress-related health problems improve after performing kind acts. Helping reverses feelings of depression, supplies social contact, and decreases feelings of hostility and isolation that can cause stress, overeating, ulcers, etc. Helping can enhance our feelings of joyfulness, emotional resilience, and vigor. An increased sense of self-worth, greater happiness, and optimism, as well as a decrease in feelings of helplessness and depression, is achieved.[6]

Although there are numerous examples of acts of kindness, we will cover volunteering, synergy, practicing generosity, and practicing mercy.

VOLUNTEER

Volunteering is a focused way of helping others. Volunteers usually work under the "umbrella" of an organization or agency like a church, Habitat for Humanity, the PTA, United Way, Girl Scouts, or Goodwill to help those in need—from those who are disabled to victims of disaster, from wayward youth to struggling seniors...and millions in between. In the United States alone, there are more than thirty-five thousand charitable organizations, many of which are focused locally, some nationally, and some internationally.

In the book *Helping You Is Helping Me*, published by World Vision (one of the largest international Christian relief and development agencies in the world), Ken Wilson and Virgil Gulker describe seven benefits of volunteering:[7]

1. Volunteers feel better—physically and about themselves. They may derive a sense of satisfaction from showing others in need that someone cares.

2. Volunteers may experience a sense of significance, or fulfillment as a result of helping others even a few hours per week.

3. Volunteering provides a context in which you can expand your network of friends and even potential new employment opportunities.

4. Volunteering is a way to expand your interests or discover new abilities.

5. Volunteering can provide a way to turn insights from your own adversity into help for somebody else who may be facing something similar.

6. Volunteering can help you view your own issues or problems from a different frame of reference.

7.   Volunteering provides an opportunity to learn from others, including those you help, and from your partners in the helping effort.

Regardless of how it is achieved, volunteering has such a positive health impact that it has been associated with improved life expectancy. One abstract reported by Dr. Linda P. Fried and others evaluated whether a program designed for older volunteers led to short-term health improvements. The report suggested that one research group found that volunteers aged fifty-five to eighty-five years who participated in two or more volunteer activities per week had a 63 percent lower mortality rate than non-volunteers.[8]

For further information about the science behind the health benefits of altruism, read Stephen G. Post's latest book *The Science of Altruism and Health: It's Good to Be Good* for the most recent findings.

SYNERGIZE

Rugged individualism and competition may have built this nation, but cooperation is healthier in terms of establishing and maintaining the supportive personal relationships that contribute to the good of others and to better health for those who help.

Let's face it; when you feel like you always have to compete with and compare yourself with others, there's a background tension, like background noise from a radio or stereo set. Your anxiety is elevated; stress is your constant companion. Since your self-esteem is linked to "winning" (and "losing" is therefore a threat), your insecurity may be off the chart. Psychologically speaking, though a little competition can keep you sharp, too much for too long can wear you down and keep you down. Physically speaking, the "fight or flight" mode this situation creates is detrimental to your health in many ways. The longer it lasts, the worse the impact. Relationally, it's hard to maintain positive and productive relationships with those whom you distrust or fear, or view as obstacles, rivals, or opponents.

The most effective way to help others as a part of any group—religious or otherwise—involves synergy, from the Greek word *synergos,* which means "working together." Synergy occurs in helping situations when the total effect is greater than the sum of the individual efforts. For example, in my work with the Christian Medical & Dental Associations, I (Dave) have participated in several short-term medical/dental missions. It is truly amazing to see how a group of twelve to twenty individuals, many of them unknown to each other when a project begins, can achieve far more in a few days of working together, even under difficult conditions, than could possibly have been achieved had the same individuals gone to the same place, one by one, even with the same goal. One plus one is three, when you factor in the cooperation, encouragement, and mutual support that come from working together for a common purpose. Add to that the sense of celebration and satisfaction shared by participants when a project is finished, and most will say that they received far more than they gave. In fact, the most common feedback received from participants is not about the number of needy people treated or even the number of those helped who came to faith as a result. It is about the spiritual, emotional, sociological, and even sometimes physical benefits that they themselves received.

Short-term medical missions participant Sue Johnson wrote:

When I decided to go on a medical missions trip this past year, I was excited to go and minister to the people of Ghana, Africa. The really unexpected wonderful thing that happened was that I was ministered to myself. God began healing things in me that I did not even know needed healing. I thought that I relied on God daily or at least tried to. I knew Jesus at a very young age and had a close relationship with Him. As I grew up, many trials and disappointments caused me to start feeling very insecure. I found myself making many compromises that led me into a path of difficulties. God was faithful and was with me as I worked to restore my relationship with Him. Despite His faithfulness to me, I had become a highly anxious person. I struggled with many feelings of inadequacy.

I was going so fast all the time that I missed opportunities daily to hear God's voice or to touch someone's life; I was very self-reliant. The interesting thing is I did not even notice all those things until I was in Africa. Through helping others in Africa by providing medical care and spiritual guidance, my life was completely altered. The experience was difficult on some days with medical equipment failing, not having the right equipment, and especially not being able to communicate. God began stripping away my own self-reliance and making me completely dependent on Him. I began letting go of past hurts—they seemed very minor in comparison to the poverty and sickness I was seeing. I began feeling confident as though I was strong enough to do this; inadequacy just faded away as I rested in God's strength and not my own. Now that I am home, I move slower—Ghanaian time, and I take time to listen—to both God and others. I have found patience and joy to replace my anxiousness. The heavy feeling of anxiety that had been in my chest is gone. I smile quicker, talk softer, and mostly just rest in the simple love of Jesus—daily. Knowing that because of me and our team sight was restored to 30 people through cataract surgery, more than 400 pairs of glasses were dispensed, more than 1,500 people were given regular medical care, 25 surgeries for wounds and ailments were performed, and more than 90 conversions into the kingdom of God were made—knowing this gives me hope and heals me of my self-reliance, for it is only through Christ that all this happened. So I went to Africa to help the hurting there, and by helping them, by touching them, I was touched, healed, transformed. I have new zest for life and a new inner peace that cannot be measured. God's Word is the living Word, indeed, as He tells us to love one another and serve one another. Taking my eyes off of myself and serving others made me actually feel better and freer. Whatever the cause, I know that as a result of helping others I am different, better, healed.*

---

* To find out more about the work of the Christian Medical & Dental Associations, including its mission work, visit: www.cmda.org.

While synergy may seem to be a relatively modern concept (the word first appeared in use around 1660), in reality it is related to the biblical principle of the interdependence of the parts of the body of Christ (1 Cor. 12). It is also described in Ecclesiastes 4:9–12:

> Two are better than one, because they have a good return for their work: If one falls down, his friend can help him up. But pity the man who falls and has no one to help him up! Also, if two lie down together, they will keep warm. But how can one keep warm alone? Though one may be overpowered, two can defend themselves. A cord of three strands is not quickly broken.

In efforts that are aligned with God's purposes, which helping those in need surely is, it's legitimate to think of this "threefold" cord as you, the person you're helping, and God.

PRACTICE GENEROSITY

God, of course, is the ultimate Giver, as expressed in one of the Bible's best-known verses, John 3:16:

> For God so loved the world that he gave his one and only Son, that whoever believes in him shall not perish but have eternal life.

Jesus said that He "did not come to be served, but to serve, and to give his life a ransom for many" (Matt. 20:28). He had a lot to say to His followers about giving, including some things that are hard to practice.

> Freely you have received, freely give.
>
> —MATTHEW 10:8

> Give to the one who asks you, and do not turn away from the one who wants to borrow from you.
>
> —MATTHEW 5:42

> So when you give to the needy, do not announce it with trumpets, as the hypocrites do in the synagogues and on the streets, to be honored by men. I tell you the truth, they have received their

reward in full. But when you give to the needy, do not let your left hand know what your right hand is doing.

—Matthew 6:2–3

Sell your possessions and give to the poor. Provide purses for yourselves that will not wear out, a treasure in heaven that will not be exhausted, where no thief comes near and no moth destroys.

—Luke 12:33

Give, and it will be given to you. A good measure, pressed down, shaken together and running over, will be poured into your lap. For with the measure you use, it will be measured to you.

—Luke 6:38

Inherent in that last verse is what we're calling the "principle of generosity reciprocity." Generosity is circular in the economy of God. Hoard what you have, and you leave with nothing. Give it away, and you get it back with some to spare. We simply cannot outgive God, who tells us to give in order to emulate His example and as a witness to others. But isn't it possible that He commands us to practice generosity because it is good for us in more than a purely spiritual sense?

Psychologist David McClelland studied the responses of Harvard student volunteers as they watched movies of various types. Those who watched a movie of Mother Teresa working among Calcutta's poor experienced a significant increase in the content of immunoglobulin-A in their saliva. Students who watched a World War II documentary as part of the same study did not experience this benefit.[9] Since immunoglobulin-A is an antibody that protects us against viruses, the implication of this finding was that even participating in caring, compassionate acts by proxy, so to speak, is beneficial to your health. This being true, just imagine how healthful it is to actually practice generosity in person.

I (Dave) have experienced multiple benefits from giving—whether time, talents, or money. But the greatest benefits have come as a result of giving my *self* in an effort to help others in the context of ministry, most often in a support group or retreat setting. How often I've been truly amazed that, having opened a session feeling exhausted from work or other pressures of the day, I end up feeling energized, even enthused, by what I've just seen happen in somebody's life and looking forward to the opportunity to do it all again.

PRACTICE MERCY

One of the Beatitudes is, "Blessed are the merciful, for they will be shown mercy" (Matt. 5:7). Our friend and hero Dr. Paul Brand and his wife, Dr. Margaret Brand, gave the best years of their lives to the lepers of India. Himself one of the kindest, most generous and merciful people we've ever known, Dr. Paul Brand described his missionary mother, "Granny" Brand, in similar terms.

> One of my last and strongest visual memories of my mother is set in a village in the mountains she loved, perhaps the last time I saw her in her own environment. She is sitting on a low stone wall that circles the village, with people pressing in from all sides. They are listening to all she has to say about Jesus. Heads are nodding in encouragement, and deep, searching questions come from the crowd. Granny's own rheumy eyes are shining, and standing beside her I can see what she must be seeing through failing eyes: intent faces gazing with absolute trust and affection on one they have grown to love.
>
> I know that even with my relative youth and strength and all my specialized knowledge about health and agricultural techniques, I could never command that kind of devotion and love from these people. They are looking at a wrinkled old face, but somehow her shrunken tissues have become transparent and she is all lambent spirit. To them, she is beautiful.[10]

The merciful love this woman showed these poor and desperate people came back to her manifold, not just in mercy shown to her, but also in devotion. The same was true of her son, who passed away in 2003 and whose memorial services were attended by a multitude of notables and needy alike. Helping others, the hallmark of his life, had made his a happy and fulfilling life indeed.

SIMPLE HEALTH

How about you? To review the health benefits of helping others, keep in mind that anything that improves your health physically, emotionally, socially, or spiritually improves your health in all arenas.

In relation to *kindness*, recall for a moment how it felt when you helped another person. Check all of the following that you have experienced as a result of doing so:

- ☐ Increased sense of happiness

- ☐ A positive physical "high"

- ☐ Energized

- ☐ Enthused

- ☐ Less depressed

- ☐ Less stressed

- ☐ More peaceful or calm

- ☐ Less conscious of my own problems

- ☐ Less aware of my own aches and pains

- ☐ Felt better about myself

- ☐ Grateful for what I have

- ☐ Felt more in touch with my spiritual self

- ☐ Felt that my sense of calling to help had been confirmed

If you want to *volunteer*, here are a few things to ask yourself before you pick up the phone:

- What do I like to do?

- What skills do I have that might be valuable to a charitable organization?

- What kind of organization (religious or secular, for example) would I want to work with?

- How much time can I give?

- Can I be reimbursed for any of my expenses?

In terms of *synergism*, ask yourself:

- Am I a good team player?

- Do I see the additional value of what I might accomplish as a part of a group versus trying to do something by myself?

- Am I committed to group or individual goals?

- Can I handle conflicts related to group goals I may not share?

- Do I really believe that one plus one is more than two within a cooperative relationship?

In terms of *giving*, solicitations are numerous. How will you decide what individuals or groups to support? Check as many of the following that apply, then take whatever action may be required:

☐ I give to anyone who asks, just as Jesus said.

☐ I have a budget for giving and use it as my guide in terms of limits.

☐ I stay informed about the charities I support.

☐ I keep good records of my donations.

☐ I know how much of what I give is really tax deductible.

☐ I keep informed about any matching gifts my donations might qualify for.

☐ When solicitors call, I tell them that I already have a giving plan.

☐ I have a tax-wise plan for the larger donations I plan to make to my favorite charities.

I try to express mercy to those in need in the following ways:

1. _____

2. _____

3. _____

My plan to change or improve the way I help others, for their sake and my own, is as follows:

My Plan

Within the next month, I will:

1. _____

2. _____

3. _____

Within the next three months, I will:

1. _____

2. _____

3. _____

Within six months, I will:

1.   _____

2.   _____

3.   _____

Chapter 10

Discover Your Purpose

Formulating Your Life's Mission Statement—
and Then Following It

The mass of men lead lives of quiet desperation.
—Henry David Thoreau

Once upon a time, a special Person walked on Planet Earth. He did *not* live a life of quiet desperation because He knew the answers to life's most important questions. As a result of knowing these answers, Jesus' life had so much meaning that when He died at a relatively young age, He could say, "It is finished," when most humans say as they depart this life, "It is over." In the original Greek, the meaning of His words is even more forceful: "It is complete, or fulfilled." In other words, Jesus was saying, "I have fulfilled the reason for which I came into this world."

The rest of us lesser humans could do less; we surely could never do more.

The world has been astounded at the success of Rick Warren's book *The Purpose-Driven Life: What on Earth Am I Here For?*, which, at this writing, has sold more than twenty *million* copies worldwide. But in reality we should not be surprised, for this book addresses the three most basic questions of human existence:

SIMPLE HEALTH

1. Why am I here?
2. Where am I going?
3. What is my mission in life?

We'll use these questions to guide us through this chapter, because the net result of how we answer them will affect our sense of personal meaning, our health, our well-being, and our happiness in life.

MEANING AND HEALTH

In terms of health, your sense of meaning in life significantly impacts the degree to which you will be able to experience optimal health or wholeness. Your physical health will be enhanced, and even if it should fail, your overall sense of wellness, or wholeness, can remain intact—if you enjoy the confidence that your life is, and has been, worthwhile. Psychologically, you will experience greater inner peace or serenity (and therefore less distress), because when you are sure your life has meaning, you can discard the need to somehow prove your worth. Sociologically, your mutually beneficial relationships will be among the sources of your greatest long-term satisfaction in life. Your life will be an oasis of strength, encouragement, and refreshment to many, as theirs will be to you. Spiritually, your soul will be able to rest in the knowledge that you are accepted, indeed loved, by the almighty God, who made you who you are and put you where you've been according to His great overarching purpose for everything, and who will welcome you into His presence when He decides it is time for you to step from time into eternity.

Our own personal experience and our observation of many others leave no question that people with a strong sense of meaning are healthier, in a broad sense, and many of them live longer than their contemporaries who do not share this characteristic. Scientific evidence is also beginning to show this to be true. In an interview with *Science and Spirit* magazine, Duke University sociologist Linda George said, "Researchers in the positive psychology movement have found that the most psychologically healthy members of the population believe life has purpose and meaning. This ties in very much with research on how religion affects health. I see people coming to recognize that having sustained meaning and purpose is an important component of thriving as human beings."[1]

There is, in fact, evidence that a sense of meaning may boost one's immune system, which is the body's primary means of protecting and healing itself. When Julienne E. Bower, PhD, and colleagues at the University of California, Los Angeles, studied forty-three women who had just lost a close relative to breast cancer, they found that those who placed the most importance on cultivating relationships, personal development, and striving for meaning in life had higher numbers of natural killer cells (a type of immune cell that fights off infections and diseases such as cancer). And over a four-week period, women who came to see these goals as more important had an improvement in their immune function.[2]

Researchers from the University of Wisconsin–Madison and Princeton University interviewed 135 women between the ages of sixty-one and ninety-one, asking them to rate their levels of two different types of positive emotional functioning: *hedonic well-being*—such as joy or happiness resulting from pleasure from experiences, and *eudaimonic well-being*—positive emotions from within, especially from the sense of being purposefully engaged with life. The researchers found that those who reported a high sense of purpose enjoyed better health. They had lower levels of stress hormones throughout the day; lower levels of substances that contribute to arthritis, hardening of the arteries, and diabetes; and higher levels of HDL cholesterol (the good kind). They were also less likely to be overweight. Those with other characteristics of eudaimonic well-being also were healthier, with lower levels of sugar in the blood or better sleep patterns.[3] Carol Ryff, UW–Madison psychology professor and lead author of the paper, described the findings:

> These preliminary findings tells us that we can achieve good health and well-being by not just eating right, exercising, and managing

SIMPLE HEALTH

stress, but by living purposeful and meaningful lives....Life enrichment may be part of what helps keep older people better regulated.[4]

To arrive at old age with a sense of meaning does not occur by chance, nor can it be manufactured (healthful as it may be) by any exercise of the mind or will. It is the net result of finding your own unique answers to the most important questions of life. As a quotient this might read: sense of purpose + direction + mission = better health, increased sense of life satisfaction, fulfillment, and even joy.

WHY AM I HERE?

In the French language, one's purpose or reason for being is called *raison d'etre*. If we exist, there is a reason. This is true for everyone, including those who deny it, those who never consider it, and even those who, for one reason or another—because they die young or before birth, or perhaps are mentally disabled—lack the capacity to consider such matters.

Some people argue that certain people are not worthy of life, but anyone who says such things does not have the divine perspective on the larger story of human history. God's perspective is that every human life, no matter how long or short, is intertwined with every other human life. This has been true since the Garden of Eden. It will continue to be true when what we call time has ended.

"You are not here just to fill space or to be a background character in someone else's movie," wrote psychologist David Niven. "Consider this: nothing would be the same if you did not exist. Every place you have ever been and everyone you have ever spoken to would be different without you. We are all connected, and we are all affected by the decisions and even the existence of those around us."[5]

I (Dave) lost a three-year-old son, who became extremely disabled before his death. Looking back now to 1978, when it happened, I can say that the value of having known and loved Jonathan and what I learned from the experience far outweigh any cost that I had to pay in

150

the process. While only God knows for sure what Jonathan's purpose in life was, without doubt his being here, if only for a little while, had something to do with what his father needed to know so he could help others find their way through their own valley of tears.

Countless others who have cared for disabled newborns, children, or adults have borne witness to the fact that while caring was demanding in every possible sense, the value of having had the opportunity to know and love that other person was beyond calculation. For in giving, we receive; in loving, we are loved. In caring for another who cannot exist without such care, we imitate the perpetual attitude of God toward us who appear to be strong but who really are weak, needy, and even disabled in more ways than we can possibly imagine, most of the time.

Having a sense of purpose that is aligned with God's overarching purposes has many values, all of them healthful. Perhaps the primary value is that purpose of this kind provides a center around which your life can be oriented. This center is like the grip on one end of a control line tethered to a gas-operated model airplane. As long as the grip is held by someone or attached to something, the plane can fly around without losing control. But cut the line or let go the grip, and that plane will fly away, free for a moment, yet destined to eventually fall to its own destruction.

When your life is centered on a purpose, you can much more easily discern which option, among the many available to you at any given moment, is better, compared with the opportunities that may be merely good. You can often even discern the best from the better. While it is never a waste of your time, energy, or talents to choose options that are merely good, your most productive and fulfilling engagements with life will be those that are most aligned with your purpose as you understand it. That happens, in part, because you will embrace them with greater passion, energy, enthusiasm, and persistence than any others.

Your decision making will be simplified in many ways by an honest answer to the question, "Will participating in this activity help me achieve my purpose in life or hinder me from doing so?" To the degree that your choices are aligned with your reason for being, your life will be more focused, effective, and satisfying long-term. Instead of rushing to and fro, like many of your peers to whom life just seems to happen, you will experience a settled sense of serenity because you've adopted a more proactive approach.

Speaking for ourselves, we write not to advance our own agendas or to achieve greater fame or fortune. We write because we must. It is the purpose for which we are here; specifically, to try to combine what we have learned with what others have to share in such a way that the final product will somehow help others toward greater wholeness. This conviction keeps us putting word after word on page after page until another book is born. And then, if our work really does help someone, we experience a great sense of fulfillment and satisfaction that the work was worthwhile.

It is possible that you have never tried to define your own purpose, that you have no clear answer to the question "Why am I here?" If you don't know or find it hard to respond in a sentence or two, a good place to start is by trying to discern your core values. Perhaps the following exercise will help. Complete the self-evaluation below by placing an "X" over the spot on each line that best describes your true beliefs or values, keeping in mind that there is no right or wrong answer in any case—only an estimation of your values at this moment:

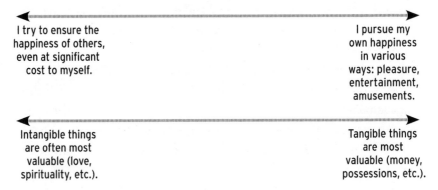

I try to ensure the happiness of others, even at significant cost to myself.

I pursue my own happiness in various ways: pleasure, entertainment, amusements.

Intangible things are often most valuable (love, spirituality, etc.).

Tangible things are most valuable (money, possessions, etc.).

I love to give away
what I have.

I save as much as
possible; I may
need it later.

I find it easy to
forgive others.

I carry grudges
for a long time.

I put the needs of
others ahead of my
own.

I take care of
myself so no one
else will have to.

Relationships are
most important to
me.

Achievements are
most important
to me.

I volunteer in my
spare time.

My spare time is
spent in pursuit
of pleasure.

I am content with
the way things are.

I'm always
striving for
something more.

I participate in
activities related to
personal growth.

I rarely try to
learn or do
something new.

I believe meaning
can be found in
most things.

Most things seem
pointless or futile
to me.

There is an
overarching
purpose to life.

Most things
happen by
chance.

My destiny is
defined by God.

I am the master
of my own
destiny.

Review your choices with these questions in mind:

1. Which questions received your most extreme responses (to the left or right)? _____

2. If there is a pattern in your most extreme responses, try to give that pattern a name. Ask yourself why you value or care so much about these things. (For example, are most of them oriented toward the needs of others, your own interests or needs, your personal pleasure or satisfaction, or positive emotions from being engaged with life?) Complete this sentence: The reason I care so much about _____ is: _____

3. Use these insights to begin drafting your statement of purpose. For example, you might say: "The reason I'm here is to help others, as much as possible, because of the way others have helped me." We'll return to this theme later in this chapter. For now, the draft of your purpose statement is: The reason I'm here is (or my purpose in life is): _____

Note: Your purpose statement can be very brief, since it is a general guide that will express itself in various ways, depending on the context. Its main function is to help you stay centered, or to put it another way, to provide a "plumb line" by which to judge whether what you're doing (or thinking of doing) is properly aligned with what you value most.

Of all the people who ever lived, Jesus was most sure of why He was here—to seek and to save those who were lost in their sin (Luke 19:10). He expressed this, in various ways, multiple times in the New Testament. Here are a few examples:

> The Spirit of the Lord is on me, because he has anointed me to preach good news to the poor. He has sent me to proclaim freedom for the prisoners and recovery of sight for the blind, to release the oppressed, to proclaim the year of the Lord's favor.
>
> —LUKE 4:18–19

The Son of Man did not come to be served, but to serve, and to give his life as a ransom for many.

—MATTHEW 20:28

I must preach the good news of the kingdom of God to the other towns also, because that is why I was sent.

—LUKE 4:43

For I have come down from heaven not to do my will but to do the will of him who sent me.

—JOHN 6:38

For this reason I was born, and for this I came into the world, to testify to the truth. Everyone on the side of truth listens to me.

—JOHN 18:37

The thief comes only to steal and kill and destroy; I have come that they may have life, and have it to the full.

—JOHN 10:10

A sense of purpose provides a reference point for navigating life, just as the North Star is the key to navigating the seas with a sextant. Still, your sense of purpose is a general guide. You still need to know where you're going, for this helps you establish more specific objectives or goals along the way. The second step toward finding meaning in life is discovering your own unique answer to the question: Where am I going?

WHERE AM I GOING?

In *The 7 Habits of Highly Effective People,* Stephen R. Covey states: "To begin with the end in mind means to start with a clear understanding of your destination. It means to know where you're going so that you better understand where you are now and so that the steps you take are always in the right direction."[6]

What do you want to accomplish in the time you've been given to live here on earth? Or to put it another way, when you reach the end of your life, what would you need to see, looking back, to consider your life successful?

Write your answer here:

_____

_____

_____

_____

This is your primary and most important goal. It is already guiding you in a certain direction, even if you've never written it down. But until you verbalize it, the pursuit of less important goals may drain your energies and resources because you sometimes go in directions you might not choose if you kept your goals in mind. (If you can't define your primary goal at this point, just come back to it later.) Secondary goals can contribute to your success if they are aligned with your primary goal.

Sometimes a believer's primary goal is best expressed in a verse from the Scriptures. In this case, it is called a "life verse." For example, when I (Dave) entered the ministry in 1974, I found a passage that seemed to summarize the goal of my life at that point:

> I want to know Christ and the power of his resurrection and the fellowship of sharing in his sufferings, becoming like him in his death, and so, somehow, to attain to the resurrection from the dead.
> —Philippians 3:10–11

In 1974 this verse expressed the deepest desire of my heart, though I didn't know then what the cost might be for God to help me reach the goal. Another verse from Philippians has been the "life verse" of many people: "I can do everything through him who gives me strength" (Phil. 4:13).

LIFE VERSES

You may have a "life verse" from the Scriptures that you embraced some time ago, though this type of goal is often not word for word, but an adaptation. For example, were you to wish to hear the Lord's words, when all is said and done, "Well done, good and faithful servant," then you might say, "My goal in life is to hear the words, 'Well done, good and faithful servant.'" Or to put this thought even more succinctly, you might say, "My goal is to have someone write on my gravestone, 'Here lies a faithful man (or woman).'"

Listed below are a few other Scriptures often used in this sense. If you want to find your own, read through the New Testament, especially the Gospels and the writings of the apostle Paul, and you'll find many. The Old Testament also contains many potential "life verses" that will summarize your ultimate life's goal.

Speaking of Paul, among New Testament characters besides Jesus, he was probably the most goal-driven.

> I press on to take hold of that for which Christ Jesus took hold of me....I do not consider myself yet to have taken hold of it. But *one thing I do: Forgetting what is behind and straining toward what is ahead, I press on toward the goal* to win the prize for which God has called me heavenward in Christ Jesus.
>
> —Philippians 3:12–14, emphasis added

In another place, Paul says:

> Do you not know that in a race all the runners run, but only one gets the prize? Run in such a way as to get the prize. Everyone who competes in the games goes into strict training. They do it to get a crown that will not last; but we do it to get a crown that will last forever. Therefore I do not run like a man running aimlessly; I do not fight like a man beating the air. No, I beat my body and make it my slave so that after I have preached to others, I myself will not be disqualified for the prize.
>
> —1 Corinthians 9:24–27

An Old Testament verse that captures the goal of many households is:

As for me and my household, we will serve the LORD.

—JOSHUA 24:15

Sometimes preachers find their goal expressed in Paul's admonition to Timothy:

Preach the Word; be prepared in season and out of season; correct, rebuke and encourage—with great patience and careful instruction.

—2 TIMOTHY 4:2

In another similar admonition, the apostle exhorts Timothy:

And the things you have heard me say in the presence of many witnesses entrust to reliable men who will also be qualified to teach others.

—2 TIMOTHY 2:2

If you didn't define your goal earlier, and this gives you some ideas on how to proceed, go back and do that before you continue reading.

Your level of success in achieving your goals will involve reaching certain objectives along the way, but objectives are not the same as goals. A professional golfer might say: "My *goal* is to win this tournament by completing all the required holes with a score lower than everyone else's score." As he hits the ball on hole number one on day number one of the tournament, the golfer's *objective* is to complete the first round with the lowest possible score he can manage *on that day*. His even more immediate objective at that moment is to achieve the best possible score he can manage on that day *on that particular hole*.

Many people never seem to stop long enough to consider their goals. They just pursue whatever comes up next, as if life were a shooting gallery with targets passing one by one. Knock down one; get ready for the next until you run out of ammunition or time. So day by day, month by month, year by year, life passes before them, and then the game ends. Of all the problems with this approach, the main one is that in everything that happens these people are passive, not proactive, participants. They don't define the targets; they only get to shoot at them. As a result, while they may make a lot of great shots and have a lot of fun, there is often no real coherence between what they've accomplished, their core values, and their purpose in being here. Looking back, they realize too late that much of what they did was a waste of time and energy that they can never recoup.

Some people think they are goal-oriented, yet their life is one never ending rush-rush-rush, trying to achieve objectives that are actually established for them by others whose approval they need or value. Achieving objectives set by others can bring a certain satisfaction, but it is more or less short-lived, because sooner or later it becomes apparent that the actual goals were someone else's goals, not necessarily something they would have chosen.

DISCERNING YOUR GOALS

(Remember, a goal is attained by long-term effort; objectives are like mile-markers along the way.)

You have already considered your values in the first section. The primary direction of your life is controlled by your goals—long and short term. These cannot conflict with your core values or your statement of purpose, or you will experience significant anxiety even if you don't recognize the source.

To identify your true goals, answer each of the following questions with a score of 0-10 (0 being "does not apply to me," and 10 being "always true of me"):

1. My goal is to become as self-sufficient as possible. _____

2. My goal is to give everything away before I die. _____

3. I want to achieve something noteworthy that is recognized. _____

4. I desire most that my life would honor God. _____

5. I want to even accounts with my adversaries before I go. _____

6. I want to somehow make the world a better place. _____

7. My goal is to become a member of a really significant group. _____

8. I want to be viewed as the world's expert in my chosen field. _____

9. I want to become president of the company for which I work. _____

10. I want to accumulate enough wealth that I won't have to worry. _____

11. I want to experience excellent physical health as long as possible. _____

12. I want to hear the Lord say, "Well done, good and faithful servant." _____

13. I want my family and friends to remember me fondly._

    _____

14. Other—My greatest goal in life is: _____

_____

Find the three or four goals you rated highest. If there is a pattern or if these can be summarized in a single sentence, write it below.

My most important goal in life is _____

_____

Note: Your most important goal will be a more powerful motivator if it is stated positively. For example, "to honor God in all I say and do" is more positive than "to never disappoint God in anything I say or do."

Having stated your goal, now define your objectives by establishing some specific long-term (ten-year), medium-term (five-year), and shorter-term objectives. For example, if your goal is to become as wealthy as possible within the foreseeable future, you might write:

- My ten-year objective is to be able to sell the business, retire young, and play golf every day that I don't go fishing.

- My five-year objective is to purchase as many of my competitors as possible.

- My three-year objective is to make my business the leader in its field.

- My one-year objective is to hire a marketing director who will take us to the next level.

- My one-month objective is to turn the cash flow positive by making major personnel changes.

- This week I will pray every day for guidance about the decisions that must be made.

Obviously, if your primary goal is, at the end of your life, to be found faithful by God, your objectives will be much different from those just listed. Goals are unique to each person; objectives are likewise unique.

Write the components of your plan to reach your primary goal here:

Ten-year objective

SIMPLE HEALTH

Five-year objective
Three-year objective
One-year objective
One-month objective
One-week objective
Today my goal is:

Filling this out may take some careful consideration. You may need to take some time away by yourself to work through the process. But if you have never done this before, the value of knowing your objectives will far outweigh the investment of your time and energy. To make our point, after you have completed this exercise, stop, take a deep breath, and see how much your anxiety has decreased now that you actually know what you want to accomplish. It will be like setting up your own target in a shooting gallery instead of waiting for another one to appear without warning.

We believe that becoming a goal-oriented person will enhance your health by promoting positive factors already described in this book and also by diminishing unhealthy factors:

- Your new sense of direction will greatly diminish your anxiety and bring a greater sense of integrity (an undivided self) than before.

- Your new sense of direction will make decision making easier, greatly reducing your sense of feeling torn between competing demands and opportunities, and guilty when you have to say no.

- You will have more energy, enthusiasm, and even passion to invest day by day in moving toward your objectives as opposed to the boredom or "chronic fatigue" experienced by many.

- You will have, perhaps for the first time in a long time, a sense of "margin" in terms of time, energy, and resources.

- You will experience fulfillment, even joy, as you reach objectives that are aligned with both your personal goals and the ultimate purposes of God.

SIMPLE HEALTH

WHAT IS MY MISSION IN LIFE?

Your sense of purpose is your overarching guide. Your goal is your long-term target. Your mission defines the specific task or tasks that have been entrusted to you. The word for this, in a more or less religious sense, is *calling* or *vocation*. As we said earlier in this book, one does not have to be a minister or missionary to have a sense of mission. One only needs to feel called to do whatever he or she is doing.

In the history of humanity, every man or woman who accomplished anything of significance in his or her field had this in common—a single-minded focus on fulfilling his or her mission. This was especially true of Jesus, whose mission of redeeming a fallen race was so compelling that when Peter, His disciple, proclaimed that the Lord would not suffer and die as He had predicted, Jesus said, "Get behind me, Satan! You are a stumbling block to me; you do not have in mind the things of God, but the things of men" (Matt. 16:23). Jesus set His face to go to Jerusalem, knowing full well what would happen there. Even His best friends could not talk Him out of it.

Since the publication of Stephen R. Covey's book *The 7 Habits of Highly Effective People*, much has been made of the importance of a mission statement to the success of organizations or families. But a similar process can be applied to individuals. Good mission statements include at least three elements:

1. They describe a reason for being, which is often oriented toward addressing a need of some kind.

2. They describe what the group (or individual) is doing or plans to do to address the need.

3. They identify core values or principles that guide their attempt to fulfill their mission.

An organizational mission statement might go like this:

The mission of our group is to assist young people in making health-enhancing physical, psychological, social, and spiritual decisions so they will be able to accomplish their greatest potential as adults, parents, and future contributors to our society.

Try using the information you have already developed in this chapter to create your own personal mission statement, which for Dave might go like this:

> My mission is to bind up the brokenhearted in Jesus' name, regardless of the cost, so they will be able to comfort others in a similar way.

Harold's mission statement might go like this:

> My mission is to serve God using my ability to do research and teach in the area of religion and health, and to be the voice of those who are sick who cannot speak for themselves.

There is no right or wrong way to state your mission. The important thing is that you do engage in the process of trying to state it, however, since once you do so, you will have a far clearer idea of which tasks are really worth working on. Not only so, but when you actually have fulfilled your mission and it's time to pass through the door we call death, you will be able to echo the words of Jesus, "It is finished," because you will have accomplished the task that only you could accomplish.

Write your mission statement here:

_____

_____

_____

_____

_____

We believe that if you wholeheartedly pursue this mission, you will be healthier and happier while doing so, and when you are finished, you will have a greater sense of meaning, fulfillment, and joy than you would have had otherwise.

We suggest that you keep these things in mind as you seek greater meaning in your life:

1. Do not allow others to define your purpose, goals, or mission. Many will try, some of them with the most seemingly innocuous motives. For example, some "get-rich-quick" infomercial may propose that your purpose is to buy a particular package to achieve wealth.

2. Don't allow others to distract or discourage you, even your family and best friends. You may even decide to keep your vision for life to yourself, since some may tell you that your goals or dreams are outrageously impractical or even impossible.

3. Do not try to create meaning. God is the only true source of meaning. Your true meaning comes from knowing Him and especially from knowing that He loves you. We can rest and take refuge in knowing this eternal reality, but we cannot add or detract from it by any human effort. Many people, especially those who have experienced trials and adversity, try to resurrect some meaning from these by establishing an organization whose mission is to help their fellow strugglers. The mission is good. The attempt to resurrect meaning is futile, however, because only God can resurrect something. In order to redeem good from evil, all we have to do is align by faith our efforts with His purposes, in which case He will use us to achieve His good pleasure to turn the purposes of the evil one on their heads. This is the core concept of redemption,

whether we speak of it globally or in a personal sense. Anyone can be called to this ultimate mission.

4. Do not be guilt-driven. The "purpose-driven" life is a good concept on the surface, but the most effective followers of Christ are not driven but called, even wooed, first by His love and compassion, and then by His example. Effective followers freely choose to emulate once they understand that they really can do so in the power of His Spirit. Guilt-driven service, whatever it may achieve, is not consistent with God's true calling, which is that you may experience real life to the full by giving it up to Him.

    If service to God is driven by guilt, it can be destructive to one's health. A doctor friend shared how one patient, who at the time was a seminary student, "...felt called to be an evangelist to a neighborhood near where he lived. In that service he was guilt driven by the thought that those he wasn't reaching or couldn't reach were going to hell and that the loss of their souls was his responsibility, his fault, and his failing." The doctor recalled, "In the midst of this intense and stressful situation he developed high blood pressure for the first time in his life. It was only when he came to the realization that the responsibility for those souls was actually and primarily God's and that God could use other individuals and situations to save those people that the student's blood pressure normalized without medication. He was trying to carry a burden that he was never meant to carry."

5. Seek to be presence-driven or, even better, presence-seeking, because the latter must precede the former if it is to be truly effective. As our good friend Dr. Jim Dill said, "A presence-seeking life in effect is fulfilling the first great commandment—to love God with all our

heart, soul, mind, and strength. A presence-driven life would then represent the outworking of that presence-seeking! The changes in us as we seek God's presence will overflow into our earthly relationships, resulting in our loving others as ourselves in our family, church, and workplace. We can only truly serve God with our whole hearts if our service is an overflow of that relationship and we come to see others as He sees them and cares for them. In that context our spiritual and 'natural' gifts are important. The things we like to do and are good at are the exact things that God is likely to use to achieve His purposes through us."

So, in relation to the questions of purpose, direction, and mission, what's your plan? Whatever it is, we guarantee that when you have a sense of purpose, a direction governed by reasonable goals, and a sense of mission that are all aligned with God's will and oriented toward the needs of others, you will *never lack opportunities* to use your time, talents, and resources in His service.

Complete the following relating to your purpose, direction, and mission.

My Plan

Short-term, in relation to my purpose, my plan is:

1. _____

2. _____

3. _____

Short-term, in relation to my direction, my plan is:

1. _____

2. _____

3. _____

Short-term, in relation to my mission, my plan is:

1. _____

2. _____

3. _____

Medium-term, in relation to my purpose, my plan is:

1. _____

2. _____

3. _____

Medium-term, in relation to my direction, my plan is:

1. _____

2. _____

3. _____

SIMPLE HEALTH

Medium-term, in relation to my mission, my plan is:

1. _____

2. _____

3. _____

Long-term, in relation to my purpose, my plan is:

1. _____

2. _____

3. _____

Long-term, in relation to my direction, my plan is:

1. _____

2. _____

3. _____

Long-term, in relation to my mission, my plan is:

1. _____

2. _____

3. _____

Chapter 11

Practice Your Faith
Connecting With the Creator of the Universe

I am come that they might have life, and that they
might have it more abundantly.

—JOHN 10:10, KJV

A grandfather was walking through his yard when he heard his
granddaughter repeating the alphabet in a tone of voice that
sounded like a prayer. When he asked her what she was doing, the
little girl explained: "I'm praying, but I can't think of exactly the
right words, so I'm just saying all the letters, and God will put them
together for me, because He knows what I'm thinking."

Connecting with our Creator through prayer, Bible reading, worship, and fellowship with other Christians is one of the greatest things
we can do to improve our health and well-being. Most people have
certain personal preferences in terms of how they express their faith.
Some view faith as a more or less private matter. Others find it most
meaningful to express their faith in public settings.

How do you personally connect with your Creator? We have
designed the following quiz to help you discern your own preferred
style before you read through the rest of this chapter. We'll return to
discuss the implications of your responses at the end of the chapter.

SIMPLE HEALTH

Instructions: On the continuums below, place a check mark at the point that best describes your preferred style of faith expression at this point in time:

1. I experience a sense of worship most fully in a...

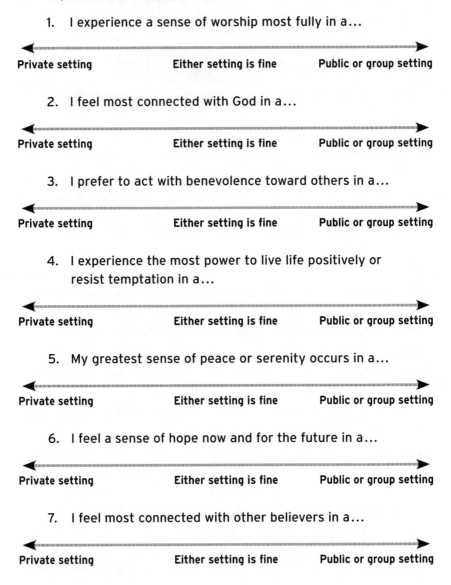

Private setting   Either setting is fine   Public or group setting

2. I feel most connected with God in a...

Private setting   Either setting is fine   Public or group setting

3. I prefer to act with benevolence toward others in a...

Private setting   Either setting is fine   Public or group setting

4. I experience the most power to live life positively or resist temptation in a...

Private setting   Either setting is fine   Public or group setting

5. My greatest sense of peace or serenity occurs in a...

Private setting   Either setting is fine   Public or group setting

6. I feel a sense of hope now and for the future in a...

Private setting   Either setting is fine   Public or group setting

7. I feel most connected with other believers in a...

Private setting   Either setting is fine   Public or group setting

8. I prefer my charitable giving to occur in a...

Private setting   **Either setting is fine**   **Public or group setting**

9. I am inspired and enabled to help others most effectively in a...

Private setting   **Either setting is fine**   **Public or group setting**

10. I am encouraged or strengthened during times of adversity in a...

Private setting   **Either setting is fine**   **Public or group setting**

11. I am able to confess my sins and feel forgiven most easily in a...

Private setting   **Either setting is fine**   **Public or group setting**

12. I feel most spiritually secure or accepted in a...

Private setting   **Either setting is fine**   **Public or group setting**

13. I am able to express my deepest concerns, including my doubts and fears, in a...

Private setting   **Either setting is fine**   **Public or group setting**

14. I feel that I can know God personally and am personally known by God in a...

Private setting   **Either setting is fine**   **Public or group setting**

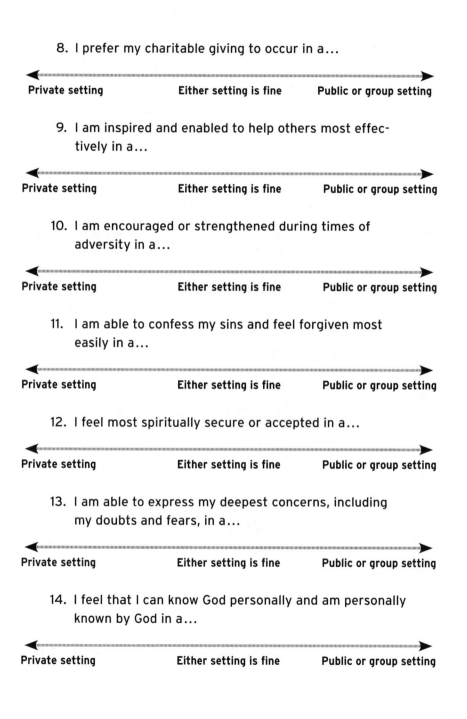

15. Life seems to make more sense in a...

◀━━━▶

Private setting   **Either setting is fine**   **Public or group setting**

16. I am able to more easily accept my mortality in a...

◀━━━▶

Private setting   **Either setting is fine**   **Public or group setting**

17. Prayer means the most to me when it occurs in a...

◀━━━▶

Private setting   **Either setting is fine**   **Public or group setting**

18. I benefit more from reading devotional material or hearing messages in a...

◀━━━▶

Private setting   **Either setting is fine**   **Public or group setting**

19. I am able to observe various rituals of faith more meaningfully in a...

◀━━━▶

Private setting   **Either setting is fine**   **Public or group setting**

20. I am able to rise above (transcend) my problems more effectively in a...

◀━━━▶

Private setting   **Either setting is fine**   **Public or group setting**

Review your responses. If there is a pattern, describe it here:

My personal preference in relation to expressing my faith tends

to be _____

_____

Assuming a pattern exists before you read this chapter, describe the effect you think your tendencies might have on the potential health benefits of practicing your faith:

_____

_____

_____

FAITH AND YOUR PHYSICAL HEALTH

Many scientific studies have found a positive correlation between religious practices, especially church attendance, and better physical health.

Here's some information on this from a fact sheet prepared by Harold on research related to faith, prayer, and health.

Religion and blood pressure

- There was a 40 percent reduction in diastolic hypertension (high blood pressure) among those who both attend religious services weekly and pray or read the Bible daily.[1]

Religion and coronary artery disease mortality

- There was a 20 percent reduction in mortality from coronary artery disease among religiously active men in Israel, after controlling for multiple risk factors; ten thousand Israeli men were followed for twenty-three years.[2]

Religious involvement and cancer

- Among women with breast cancer, those not affiliated with any religious organization were over four times more likely to die during follow-up, compared to women with any religious affiliation. (Nonreligious African American women were over ten times more likely to die.)[3]

- Persons who attended religious services at least weekly and who exercised regularly, didn't smoke, and got seven to eight hours of sleep a night, were 76 percent less likely to die of cancer during a thirteen-year follow-up.[4]

Religious attendance and immune function

- Weekly attendees at religious services have a 49 percent lower likelihood of having high IL-6 levels (i.e., impaired immune function) (42 percent lower after controlling for age, sex, race, education, chronic illness, physical functioning).[5]

- Attending religious services more than once a week was associated with a 66 percent reduction in likelihood of having a high IL-6 level and 68 percent reduction in mortality.[6]

- Women with metastatic breast cancer who have greater religious expression have higher numbers of natural killer cells.[7]

- Long-term survivors with AIDS are more religious and have lower serum cortisol levels (a hormone that may impair immune function).[8]

- HIV-positive men with greater religious involvement have higher CD-4 counts (immune cells that protect people from infection, cancer, etc.).[9]

- Private religious practice predicts healthier cortisol rhythms among women with fibromyalgia.[10]

Strong religious beliefs and surgery

- Death rates are fourteen times lower for older adults during the first six months after undergoing open-heart surgery among those with both high social support and high religious coping.[11]

- Stronger religious beliefs are associated with fewer complications and shorter hospital stays among patients undergoing cardiac surgery.[12]

Need for health services

- Patients not affiliated with a religious denomination spent an average of twenty-five days at Duke Hospital, compared to eleven days for those with a religious affiliation.[13]

- African Americans who prayed, meditated, and read the Bible a lot during hospitalization spent five days on average in long-term care settings (nursing homes) during the ten months after hospital discharge, compared to nearly fifty days for those who prayed and read the Bible a small amount.[14]

Prayer and longevity

- There is a 47 percent increase in risk of dying during a six-year period for healthy older adults who do not pray.[15]

Religion, faith, and longevity

- There is a 46 percent reduction in death rates for weekly attendees at religious services compared to those attending less than weekly; a 28 percent reduction after controlling for other risk factors.[16]

- There is a 34 percent reduction in death rates for women who attended religious services weekly compared to others followed for twenty-eight years.[17]

- There is a seven-year greater longevity for whites who attend religious services more than weekly compared to those who don't attend; a fourteen-year greater longevity for African Americans.[18]

Frequency of church attendance is the most common factor in studies related to faith and health, perhaps because it is easier to quantify than some other more private expressions of one's faith. But since deciding to spend more time in a church building cannot turn an unbeliever into a believer any more than spending a lot of time in a stable can make that person a horse, deciding to start attending church regularly in order to achieve better health is not the best way to use the information you're about to read. In other words, attending church with such a hidden agenda and no other reason most likely will not do you much good. On the other hand, we do hope that, if you don't currently attend church regularly, as a result of reading this chapter you will be inspired to do so as one who worships "in spirit and truth," as Jesus put it, "for they are the kind of worshipers the Father seeks" (John 4:23).

We suspect that a primary reason that church attendance and better health appear linked is because active involvement in a faith community has positive emotional, sociological, and spiritual benefits, and it often encourages a healthier lifestyle.

YOUR FAITH, YOUR HEALTH, AND YOUR DOCTOR

Studies published in the *Archives of Internal Medicine* and the *Journal of Family Practice* state that more than 80 percent of physicians surveyed thought they should be aware of a patient's religious beliefs and consider their spiritual needs in treatment.[19] However, a much smaller percentage (31 to 39 percent) agreed that doctors should inquire about patients' spiritual beliefs.[20] Less than 10 percent of doctors regularly address spiritual concerns even with patients who are terminally ill.[21] It should come as no surprise, then, that a survey of nearly two million U.S. hospital patients found that patients were often dissatisfied with the emotional and spiritual aspects of care they received.[22]

Many doctors either have no interest in or have not been trained in how to discern or respond to the spiritual needs of their patients. The Christian Medical & Dental Associations (CMDA), with which Dave has been associated for more than fifteen years, is trying to do something to change this in a variety of ways, from training medical and dental students to sponsoring workshops and seminars such as the internationally successful series "The Saline Solution." In *Practice by the Book*,[23] Drs. Gene Rudd and Al Weir suggest that Christian doctors might ask themselves, in each patient encounter, "What is God doing?" (WIGD), with the goal of opening communication channels about spiritual matters between patient and doctor. Each doctor who acknowledges spiritual needs of patients as legitimate health concerns will pursue these needs with you in a unique way. But the most important thing, if you have spiritual concerns that you think may be affecting your health, is that you communicate these in some way to your health-care provider.

FAITH AND YOUR PSYCHOLOGICAL HEALTH

Psychological factors, especially long-term emotional stress, may negatively influence physical health by affecting the immune system, the body's natural first defense against infection and other illness. This leaves you more susceptible to minor health problems such as colds or flu, and it could even in some cases influence the development of serious illnesses such as cancer or coronary heart disease. High levels of stress-related hormones, such as cortisol, epinephrine, and norepinephrine, can increase blood pressure, which may over time lead to damages in the arteries that supply blood to the heart and the brain, and even affect cholesterol deposits (plaque) in blood vessel walls. These changes can increase your risk of having a heart attack or stroke. Faith helps to diminish emotional stress through providing inner peace, hope, and optimism. Your community of faith may help reduce your stress through social support during times of need, close friendships, and access to counseling from the ministerial staff.

Studies show that people who regularly attend worship services are significantly less likely to become depressed, and those with deep faith recover from depression more quickly. Faith also helps people cope better with major life events, combating pessimism or despair that can sometimes lead to ignoring one's health, including the need for regular medical checkups.

People experiencing long-term emotional stress sometimes seek relief by cigarette smoking, alcohol or drug use, risky sexual behaviors, unhealthy eating habits, or other activities that can add to and worsen health problems. One's faith can counteract these temptations by providing alternative ways of coping with stress (prayer, talking things over with another church member) and also by observing religious teachings that help us to avoid behaviors that can negatively impact our health.

Overall, people of faith tend to experience a higher level of life satisfaction, which can affect the quality of life and may even influence their health in general.

FAITH AND YOUR SOCIOLOGICAL HEALTH

Positive and constructive relationships—whether with family or friends—promote wellness. Couples who share faith divorce less frequently because they are more likely to view their marriages as sacred, to change attitudes and behavior in order to prevent divorce, or to seek pastoral counseling when it is needed. Divorce has well-established negative results on health. One summary of the research claimed that:

> Researchers...found that premature death rates, defined as occurring between the ages of 15 and 64, "are significantly higher from

a number of diseases among divorced men and women compared to married persons the same sex and age."

After reviewing studies "based on data from the National Center for Health Statistics on all deaths that occurred in the United States for a two-year period, it was discovered that the premature death rate for divorced men due to cardiovascular disease was double that of married men, whites and non-whites alike. The premature death rate for divorced men due to stroke was double that of married men, and early death by pneumonia was more than seven times higher for white divorced men, [when] compared to their married counterparts." Premature death due to hypertension among divorced men was twice that of married men and "suicide was four times higher for divorced white men than those married."[24]

Social support from family and friends, including their "brothers and sisters" in the community of faith, can help combat the negative effects of stress, reducing the risk of depression and speeding recovery from depression when it does occur. A strong network of family and friends can support good health habits such as a healthier diet, more exercise, and better sleep. Sometimes this support is best accessed in a group setting.

Other types of faith-based support groups have greatly increased over the past several decades. The most effective groups focus on specific interests such as parenting or needs shared by those who attend, including recovery from a variety of addictions, dealing with divorce, depression, cancer, chronic pain, eating disorders, disability, or the loss of a loved one to suicide or disease. There is no doubt that the compassion and understanding you can receive from your like-minded fellow strugglers during times of acute distress, or simply to carry on with living, is health-enhancing.[25]

FAITH AND YOUR SPIRITUAL HEALTH

If you and I (Dave) could have a heart-to-heart discussion about faith and its relation to health, here's what I would want you to know.

SIMPLE HEALTH

First, I would want it to be clear that not everything you may hear in church or a religious discussion group is health-enhancing, so you need to take it "with a grain of salt," or spiritual discernment. "The truth will set you free," as Jesus said in John 8:32, and fearing God will bring "health to your body and nourishment to your bones," as Solomon said in Proverbs 3:8. But when what you hear increases your sense of guilt, judgment by humans, or feelings of abandonment or punishment by God, your risk of ill health, even death, might be increased.

A study of nearly 450 older hospitalized patients—most of them Christians—by Harold and his Duke University colleagues found that feeling alienated from God, one's religious community, or perceiving the devil as the cause of one's illness resulted in a 19 to 28 percent increased risk of dying during the subsequent two years. Evidently, the unresolved inner stress related to these religious convictions created a context for decline in health over time.[26]

Religious media personalities preaching the "health and wealth gospel" can sometimes contribute to ill health in those who listen by making claims about healing or health in general that are not supported by Scripture when taken as a whole. Listeners who "believe" and try to implement these concepts are often led down "the primrose path" of false expectations, only to be disappointed in the end when their wishes or longings for health or healing are not fulfilled. Disillusioned disciples of these false teachers often wander through the rest of their lives unnecessarily burdened by a sense of guilt that, had their "faith" only been stronger, things would have happened differently. I have personally heard the sad stories of scores, perhaps hundreds, of those whose wishes and prayers were not granted, and who then struggled mightily to put the pieces of their faith back together again.

Since 1978 when I lost my first son to disease, I have personally heard from a variety of self-proclaimed faith healers and others with supposedly inspired opinions about why Jonathan was not healed (or later, in 1986, what I needed to do in order to access God's healing power for my second son when he was ill). When you are in great distress and desperate to try almost anything, it's easy to give in to the temptation to believe such claims and follow such people unless you've been immersed for years, as I had been, in biblical teachings on a wide variety of subjects, including divine healing.

In my opinion, the Scriptures are clear that God sometimes does intervene supernaturally and restore physical health to those who are sick. Supernatural healings can be found in both Old and New Testaments. Many such healings were performed by Jesus and are recorded in the Gospels. The biblical view is, in my opinion, that God is certainly not a supernatural puppet who can be manipulated by prayer or penitence or anything at all. He does (or allows) what He does because it contributes to His overall purposes in relation to the redemption of humanity, bruised, broken, and sick as we often are. While achieving these purposes does occasionally involve restoring a person's health so he or she can continue to witness to God's existence and grace, sometimes it involves healing a person's mind or spirit or relationships even at a time when he or she may be in the process of dying. Strange as it may sound, some people are most whole (and therefore most healthy) near the end of their lives.

The practice of authentic, health-enhancing faith is not dependent on one's denomination or membership in any religious group. It does not happen through walking the aisle in a religious service or by praying a prayer at the end of an evangelistic booklet. The life of faith is not achieved by adherence to a list of "dos and don'ts" imposed by any person or group. Instead the practice of authentic faith is, to put it very simply, the overflow of a love relationship with God that is established through trusting Christ as one's personal Lord and Savior. This, therefore, is the first step toward a full and healthy life, because this relationship provides peace with God and peace in our hearts. As Proverbs 14:30 says, "A heart at peace gives life to the body."

A love relationship with God also provides the will and the ability to love and serve our fellow humans with whom we share a special sense of community in the church. The human love relationships we experience as a result encourage and empower us as we live our lives day to day, and they further enhance our relationship with God, as the benefits go round and round.

Consequently, faith is not something that ordinarily grows or finds its greatest health-enhancing expression in isolation. Yes, certain ascetics (hermit types) through the centuries have gained significant insights into the character of God and His ways in our world. But the value of their insights was that they *shared them with others.* Our observations, experience, understanding of the Scriptures, and the results of scientific research all support the idea that even though everyone has a unique style of practicing faith (as you saw in the quiz at the beginning of this chapter), the health-enhancing benefits of faith in practice are most evident when faith is practiced in both private *and* public settings. If your preferences are strongly toward the private side, a good idea would be to consider how you might add more group-oriented experiences to your practice of faith.

The most common public setting is, of course, participating in religious services. Although no one can say which part of a church service is most healthful to the body, mind, soul, or even relationally, it is likely that the effect is cumulative. The sermon may convict, inspire, or both; the music elevates the spirit, especially in the process of congregational praise and worship; and the prayers present the participants' shared confession, adoration of God, and needs and concerns together before His throne. The words of encouragement from fellow attendees is a strong reminder, week by week, that however joyful or difficult your situation may be, you are not in it alone, for as the saying goes, "joy shared is joy enhanced; sorrow shared is sorrow diminished."

The private side of faith is important, too, since authentic faith is surely not something that only happens one day a week for an hour or so. Those who have the most vibrant faith (remember that faith is primarily relational) enhance their relationship with God through private prayer or meditation on the Scriptures, reading devotional materials, or listening to inspiring music.

The net result of nurturing your faith in both private and public settings will be that you simply will not be able to keep it to yourself. I don't mean by this that all people with authentic faith become preachers, evangelists, or missionaries, only that true faith is other-directed. In other words, your concern for and involvement with others in a helping or redemptive sense will increase in a variety of ways as your faith grows. This too enhances your health, as we said in the chapter on helping others. Don't worry. You don't have to make this happen. It happens because the Spirit of God, who comes to reside within believers, is a powerful force for love, compassion, and concern, bringing refreshment to those in need. The way Jesus described it to the woman at the well was:

> Everyone who drinks this water will be thirsty again, but whoever drinks the water I give him will never thirst. Indeed, the water I give him will become in him a spring of water welling up to eternal life.
>
> —JOHN 4:13–14

Sometimes others will notice something about you—perhaps some part of the fruit of the Spirit: "love, joy, peace, patience, kindness, goodness, faithfulness, gentleness and self-control" (Gal. 5:22–23). Perhaps they will notice your uncommon hope in the face of difficulties you may be experiencing. Here is how the apostle Peter described what can happen: "But in your hearts set apart Christ as Lord. Always be prepared to give an answer to everyone who asks you to give the reason for the hope that you have. But do this with gentleness and respect" (1 Pet. 3:15).

This sense of hope that marks believers is one of the strongest antidotes to the despair, sense of futility, or loss of meaning that many without faith experience as a result of significant loss. The writer of Hebrews described this hope of believers as an "anchor for the soul" (Heb. 6:19). Instead of being tossed about by every distressing or painful event of life, believers can rest secure in knowing that although they may not understand or make sense of it all, they know the One who can speak peace to the storm. It is ultimately His story, not ours, that is the history of which our lives are a part.

This hope is not some wishful thinking concocted by the needs of weaklings who cannot face reality. It is linked to God and His promises, which are always "Yes" to those who trust in Christ. (See 2 Corinthians 1:20.) In other words, God is for us. He is on our side. All of His revealed Word whispers these words in the spiritual ears of those who can hear: "I am here. I love you. You don't need to be afraid."

The truth about faith's view of reality is that because of the love relationship we have with God through faith in Christ, we are far better equipped to face our own mortality without fear. One of the most significant results of Jesus' taking on human flesh was that "by his death he might destroy him who holds the power of death—that is, the devil—and free those who all their lives were held in slavery by their fear of death" (Heb. 2:14–15).

Making peace with reality in this way is surely one of the most health-enhancing results of authentic faith, because we know for sure that, in the words of the apostle Paul:

> When the perishable has been clothed with the imperishable, and the mortal with immortality, then the saying that is written will come true: "Death has been swallowed up in victory." "Where, O death, is your victory? Where, O death, is your sting?" The sting of death is sin, and the power of sin is the law. But thanks be to God! He gives us the victory through our Lord Jesus Christ.
>
> —1 CORINTHIANS 15:54–57

But Paul doesn't stop there, as if this sense of victory is only relevant to our own mental health or something we can just keep to ourselves. "Therefore, my dear brothers," he adds, "stand firm. Let nothing move you. Always give yourselves fully to the work of the Lord, because you know that your labor in the Lord is not in vain" (v. 58).

The bottom line of everything we've written in this entire book is that our health and, indeed, our very lives are not ends in themselves but means to an end—being steadfast, immovable, and fully engaged in the work that the Lord has entrusted to us, whatever that may be. Knowing this, and putting it into practice, is the greatest source of wholeness any human being can experience.

SUGGESTIONS FOR PRACTICING YOUR FAITH IN PRIVATE

- Understand that nurturing your relationship with God through faith in Christ will require a similar investment of time and energy as is required for the establishment, maintenance, and growth of your human relationships. It is unreasonable to expect that having come to faith you can just let the whole thing slide, as if it were a type of eternal life insurance policy to be cashed in when needed.

- Spending time alone with God in prayer or meditation on the Scriptures, which is His Word to us, or devotional materials is not complicated, and through the years many helps have been devised to assist believers in keeping this time fresh and vibrant. Many have found that listening to inspirational music is very helpful when they want to open communication with the Father.

- Recently, one of our friends, Dr. Randall Martin, developed what he calls a "prayer tool" on which you can write your requests, answers to prayer, or words of praise while coordinating these with God's promises. You can use this pocket-sized tool as a bookmark in your Bible, or carry it with you when you are walking or traveling in order to focus your prayers on specific needs or concerns you wish to bring before God.*

*For more information, visit Dr. Martin's website, www.prayertool.com.

- Keep your private devotional time personal, as it can become stale and ineffective if it is something you practice purely out of a sense of obligation. Love is heart to heart, so the best way to nurture your relationship with God is to tell Him the truth every time you meet. "Let it all hang out," for He will never be surprised by anything you say.

- The setting, timing, or your motivation will all affect the benefit you receive from time alone with God. Speaking personally, I (Dave) have had all my most significant "dialogues" with God when I was outdoors, often hiking through the wilderness. For some reason, at least for me, the Rockies, with their awesome majesty, are the perfect place for "the hound of heaven" to catch up to me and remind me of the things I need to remember. Prayer as I hike along in that setting is as near as I can come to what the apostle Paul meant by "pray without ceasing"—it's a frame of mind, like having a high-speed connection to heaven that's always on.

SUGGESTIONS FOR PRACTICING FAITH IN PUBLIC

The famous British poet John Donne once wrote, "No man is an island entire of itself, every man is a piece of the Continent..." Those words hold true within the context of anyone who practices his or her faith. Indeed, not only is there a sense of human solidarity in a global sense (especially as it relates to alienation from God as a result of sin), but there is also an even greater sense of solidarity between members of family of faith. Faith, in a biblical sense, is something that God expects us to practice not just for the benefit to ourselves, but also because its practice in a group setting has a synergistic or mutually edifying and encouraging effect.

Perhaps the phrase that most captures the importance of shared faith is "one another," which occurs more than thirty times in the

New Testament. Jesus, Paul, Peter, John, and the writer of Hebrews all use this phrase. Believers are to love, be devoted to, live in harmony with, be accepting toward, patient with, forbearing toward, forgiving toward, encouraging toward, humble toward, and hospitable toward one another. It is simply not possible to fulfill these exhortations in isolation.

The expectation was, instead, to "let us consider how we may spur one another on toward love and good deeds. Let us not give up meeting together, as some are in the habit of doing, but let us encourage one another" (Heb. 10:24–25). In another passage, Paul describes what should take place in such meetings: "Speak to one another with psalms, hymns and spiritual songs. Sing and make music in your heart to the Lord, always giving thanks to God the Father for everything, in the name of our Lord Jesus Christ" (Eph. 5:19–20).

- A public or group setting can be something as simple as a mentoring or friendship relationship with one or more people whose spiritual guidance you value. Great strength and encouragement can be gained in this semiprivate context where you can be yourself, with all your doubts, fears, temptations, and even victories over temptations, yet still be accepted as you are and as you continue to grow, because everyone involved is still in process. The mutual expression of faith in such settings usually benefits all participants.

- Many churches also sponsor small groups aimed at fellowship and spiritual growth (as opposed to support groups that are most usually focused on dealing more successfully with one or more of life's challenges). Small groups may vary greatly as to style, often related to the group's leadership. The most common of them might be geographically oriented, providing church members in the communities where they reside an opportunity to know and support each other on a more personal basis.

- The primary public gathering of your church is most likely the worship service on Sunday morning, though many churches conduct services on other days of the week for one reason or another. Also, the style of services offered at various times may differ in order to cater to the preferences of sub-groups such as youth or young adults who may prefer a contemporary style to whatever is traditional these days. Many evangelical churches also have services on Sunday and Wednesday evenings for reasons that are most likely more traditional than anything else. The main question in relation to the health-enhancing benefits of church attendance is not which style you prefer, but whether or not you attend at all. We hope that you do, or that you will start doing so, and that when you do, you'll both receive what you need and also give what you can to the others who are there with you.

EXPRESSING YOUR FAITH PRIVATELY AND PUBLICLY

When you completed the quiz at the start of this chapter, and as you've worked your way through the rest of the chapter, you have most likely realized that now would be a good time to make some improvements in the private or public expression of your faith. We trust that this realization is not motivated solely by your desire for better health, though the evidence is pretty clear that the public and private expression of faith can contribute to better health. The main question for you, personally, is whether or not you are satisfied with your faith as it now finds expression or if you think there is room for improvement. If there is room for improvement, you may benefit by completing the following:

My Plan

Within the next month, I will:

1. _____

2. _____

3. _____

Within the next three months, I will:

1. _____

2. _____

3. _____

Within the next six months, I will:

1. _____

2. _____

3. _____

Within a year, I will:

1. _____

2. _____

3. _____

HOW TO DEVELOP A PERSONAL LOVE
RELATIONSHIP WITH GOD

Establishing a love relationship with God is not as difficult as some make it seem. There really is no formula for this, though there are numerous programs available that describe "steps" or "laws" or a variety of other factors that their creators thought should be considered.

Jesus' approach was pretty simple. "Follow Me," He said. He didn't say what might lie ahead; for example, martyrdom and so forth. He just invited those listening to follow Him, wherever it might take them, and many of them did.

The same invitation exists today. Jesus came that those who choose to follow Him might experience life to the full instead of continuing unsuccessfully to try to deal with the ultimate futility of life lived outside the divine purposes for which every person was created.

John 3:16 is one of the best-known verses of the Bible: "For God so loved the world that he gave his one and only Son, that whoever believes in him shall not perish but have eternal life." This verse is part of a conversation that Jesus had with a man named Nicodemus, which led to their discussion of what being "born again" or "born from above" could possibly mean.

The question for you, and anyone considering establishing a love relationship with God through faith in Christ, is this: Are you willing to place your faith in Christ (believe in Him as Savior) instead of trying to save yourself from your sins? This is what it means to "accept" Jesus as your Savior. The next step, and one that was never left optional by Jesus when He was here in person, is: Are you willing to allow Him to be the Lord of your life? You really need to think this one through, since a lord is one who has power or control over what happens, and that power and control are not things that are easy to surrender.

If you are willing, then here is a sample prayer you might pray in your own words to begin your personal journey of faith:

Dear God,

I really want to experience life to the fullest possible measure, and I realize that I cannot do so on my own. I understand that the reason Jesus lived and died was to make it possible for me to experience this kind of life, because He paid the penalty for my sins on the cross—sins that have kept me separated from You and what You wish to give me until this moment. Right now, I am placing my faith in Him as my personal Savior, and I will seek to follow Him wherever that leads me, even beyond this life into eternity. Amen.

Conclusion

To Be Continued...by You!

We set out to help you experience a fuller and more meaningful life and, therefore, a healthier and happier life. As we said right up front, wellness is dynamic and uniquely defined by each individual. It changes with age, time, and sometimes with circumstances, but the basic principles involved are simple and inexpensive to implement. The basic principles of wellness involve more than the biological realm, but a combination of wellness in physical, emotional, sociological, and spiritual realms.

While many people today worship their bodies and strive for optimal wellness as they understand it in a purely physical or material sense, our goal throughout has been to show that illness in one arena of life affects all others, and increased wellness does the same.

The main point we wanted to communicate about health is that believers do best when they view health not as an end in itself, but as a means to an end—the greatest end being to love the Lord our God with all our hearts, souls, mind, and strength, and to love our neighbors as ourselves. (See Mark 12:30–31.) The longer you survive with health and energy to pursue this goal, the greater will be your sense of meaning and therefore your overall sense of wellness.

Of the many possible subjects we might have included, we chose eleven that more or less cover the waterfront. As you review these now, choose the three where you still need to make the most improvement. Our topics were:

SIMPLE HEALTH

1. Laugh more
2. Keep your mind active
3. Manage stress well
4. Get enough rest and exercise
5. Eat and drink healthy things
6. Be proactive about your health-care management
7. Nurture your relationships
8. Increase your happiness
9. Help somebody else
10. Discover your purpose
11. Practice your faith

My Plan

In which three arenas do you need the most improvement during the next year?

1. _____

2. _____

3. _____

If you were to begin with the arena where change is most urgently needed, it would it be:

_____

What is your plan for improvement in the next month?

1. _____

2. _____

3. _____

What is your plan for improvement in the next three months?

1. _____

2. _____

3. _____

What is your plan for improvement in the next six months?

1. _____

2. _____

3. _____

What is your plan for improvement in the next year?

1. _____

2. _____

3. _____

SIMPLE HEALTH

CHARTING YOUR PROGRESS

In the introduction, we provided a wellness quiz so you would have a baseline score by which to evaluate your progress over time. Assuming that you completed that quiz before reading the book, we include it here again so you can retake it and see how you're doing thus far.

As before, write your estimate of your current wellness quotient (using a scale of 100) in the space provided before completing the survey. We hope that your score will have improved already, but we are confident that, if you really do implement the health-enhancing principles we've presented, your overall sense of wellness will improve over time.

To your health!

—David B. Biebel
—Harold G. Koenig

WELLNESS QUIZ

Your wellness quotient estimate: _____

Before you begin the questionnaire, estimate your current wellness quotient (your current overall level of wellness) on a scale of 100, and write it on the line above. Then compare it to the total after you answer the questions.

Answer the questions below before you start reading the book. Enter one number for each question, using the scale of 1-5 below in terms of the degree to which a statement is true of you. If something is *never true*, just leave it blank or enter a zero. After answering all the questions, add your score. The total is your current "wellness quotient." See note below regarding our view of how to understand and use this score.

1   *Not usually true*
2   *Sometimes true*
3   *Maybe/can't decide*

4   *Usually true of me*
5   *Always true*

1. I enjoy a good laugh or good humor. _____

2. I exercise my mind by engaging in creative activity or problem solving. _____

3. I try to manage my stress instead of letting it manage me. _____

4. I get enough sleep and exercise. _____

5. I eat and drink healthy things, do not use tobacco, and use alcohol in moderation or not at all. _____

6. I avoid fad diets. _____

7. I try to keep my living environment as healthy as possible. _____

8. I monitor my health via various means, including regular medical and dental checkups. _____

9. I have at least one friend in whom I can confide. _____

10. I am satisfied with what I have and am thankful for it. _____

11. I find pleasure (or a sense of satisfaction) in my work. _____

12. I value my family relationships and try to protect them through faithfulness and reconciliation. _____

13. I have a sense of purpose, direction, and meaning in life. ____

14. I am a generous and kind person, concerned for those in need (humans and/or animals). _____

15. I work with others to achieve more cooperatively than we might achieve individually. _____

16. I am a happy and optimistic person, savoring life in the present tense. _____

17. My faith in God brings a sense of peace and helps me during times of adversity. _____

18. I engage in religious activities such as prayer, Bible study, devotional reading, or worship. _____

19. I have accepted my own mortality—knowing that I will someday die. _____

20. I have hope, not only in the present tense, but also a hope of eternal life when this life is over. _____

Total: My wellness quotient today is: _____

Date: _____ / _____ / _____

This is not a scientific questionnaire, just twenty questions related to wellness. We have observed that people with a score of less than 70 realize that there is room for improvement. People with scores of 70–80 have a healthy level of perceived wellness, though there is still room for improvement. People with scores of 80–90 are likely enjoying optimum wellness, while they are also most likely lifelong learners and pursuers of good health. Scores higher than 90 suggest that the individuals involved might benefit by closely reexamining the areas they scored as always true of them, with a view toward whether or not their perceptions are overly optimistic. Sometimes a trusted friend who knows you well can help with this.

Notes

Chapter 1: Laugh Yourself Healthy

1. Norman Cousins, *Anatomy of an Illness as Perceived by the Patient* (New York: W. W. Norton & Company, 1979).

2. Paul E. McGhee, PhD, "Humor and Health," HolisticOnline.com Humor, http://www.holisticonline.com/Humor_Therapy/humor_mcghee_article.htm (accessed April 26, 2005).

3. Dr. Lee Berk and Dr. Stanley Tan, "The Therapeutic Benefits of Laughter," *Humor and Health Journal* (September–October 1996).

4. "Therapeutic Benefits of Laughter," HolisticOnline.com Humor, http://www.holisticonline.com/Humor_Therapy/humor_therapy_benefits.htm (accessed April 26, 2005).

5. McGhee, "Humor and Health."

6. Ibid.

7. Ibid.

8. "Humor and Laughter: Health Benefits and Online Sources," Helpguide, http://www.helpguide.org/aging/humor_laughter_health.htm (accessed June 13, 2005).

9. Allen Klein, *The Lift-Your-Spirits Quote Book* (New York: Random House, 2001).

10. Tom Evans, "Laughter Is Good Medicine," TheIowaChannel.com, August 1, 2002, http://theiowachannel.com/health/1590024/detail.html (accessed June 29, 2005).

11. Leslie Flynn, *Serve Him With Mirth* (Grand Rapids, MI: Zondervan, 1960).

12. Chuck Swindoll, "The Winsome Witness," Crosswalk.com, http://broadcasts.crosswalk.com/ministries/insight_for_living/Article.asp?article_id=573 (accessed June 29, 2005).

Chapter 2: Exercise Your Mind

1. Dr. Gene Cohen, *The Creative Age: Awakening Human Potential in the Second Half of Life* (New York: HarperCollins, 2000).

2. J. M. Smyth, et al., "Effects of Writing About Stressful Experience on Symptom Reduction in Patients With Asthma or Rheumatoid Arthritis: A Randomized Trial," *Journal of the American Medical Association* 281(14) (April 14, 1999): 1304–1309.

3. K. Klein, and A. Boals, "Expressive Writing Can Increase Working Memory Capacity," *Journal of Experimental Psychology* 130(3) (September 2001): 520–533.

4. David Biebel, *If God Is So Good, Why Do I Hurt So Bad?* (Grand Rapids, MI: Baker Book House, 1995).

5. F. Youssef and J. I. Addae, "Learning May Provide Neuroprotection Against Dementia," *West Indian Medical Journal* 51(3) (2002): 143–147.

6. Ibid.

Chapter 3: Manage Your Stress

1. This list is based in part on an article by Bobbie Dill, BSN, RN, et al., "The Registered Nurse's Role in the Office Treatment of Patients With Histories of Abuse," *Gastroenterology Nursing* 20(5) (1997): 162–167, the official journal of the Society of Gastroenterology Nurses and Associates, Inc. (SGNA).

2. Richard A. Swenson, MD, *The Overload Syndrome* (Colorado Springs: NavPress, 1998), 14–15.

3. Ayn Rand, "Why I Like Stamp Collecting," *Minkus Stamp Journal,* 1971.

4. Bill Malone, MSW, LISW, "Get Into a Hobby: It's Good for You!", Malone Counseling and Consulting Services, LLC, http://www.canville.net/malone/getahobby.html (viewed June 30, 2005).

5. Henry David Thoreau, "Where I Lived, and What I Lived For," *Walden,* http://www.transcendentalists.com/walden_where_i_lived.htm (accessed June 30, 2005).

6. Loretta LaRoche, *Relax, You May Only Have a Few Minutes Left* (New York: Villard Books, 1998).

7. Ibid.

8. C. Krucoff, "Pump Up Your Spirit," *Raleigh News and Observer,* March 12, 1999.

9. Paul Roberts, "Goofing Off," *Psychology Today*, July/August 1995, http://cms.psychologytoday.com/articles/pto-19950701-000020.html (accessed June 30, 2005).

Chapter 4: Get Enough Exercise and Rest

1. Some of these have been adapted from Nick Nilsson, "Humor: Tenderizing Meat and Other Uses for Home Exercise Equipment," ShapeUpShop.com, www.shapeupshop.com/go/modules.php?name=News&file=article&sid=90 (accessed June 30, 2005).

2. J. L. Tanji, "The Benefits of Exercise for Women," *Clinics in Sports Medicine* 19(2) (2000): 175–185. R. S. Taylor, et al., "Exercise-Based Rehabilitation for Patients With Coronary Heart Disease: Systematic Review and Meta-Analysis of Randomized Control Trials," *American Journal of Medicine* 116(10) (2004): 682–692. S. R. Chipkin, et al., "Exercise and Diabetes," *Cardiology Clinics* 19(3) (2001): 489–505. S. J. Colcombe, et al., "Aerobic Fitness Reduces Brain Tissue Loss in Aging Humans," *Journals of Gerontology Series A-Biological Sciences & Medical Sciences* 58(2) (2000): 176–180. K. T. Lesniak and P. M. Dubbert, "Exercise and Hypertension," *Current Opinion in Cardiology* 16(6) (2001): 356–359. N. A. Sharkey, et al., "The Role of Exercise in the Prevention and Treatment of Osteoporosis and Osteoarthritis," *Nursing Clinics of North America* 35(1) (2000): 209–221. C. J. Lavie, et al., "Effects of Cardiac Rehabilitation and Exercise Training Programs in Women With Depression," *American Journal of Cardiology* 83(10) (1999): 1480–1483, A7. D. Glenister, "Exercise and Mental Health: A Review," *Journal of the Royal Society of Health* 116(1) (1996): 7–13.

3. Exercise and health "factoids" are from http://www.coloradohealthsite.org/exercise/exercise_def.html and other online sources.

4. "Stretching Exercises to Increase Flexibility," WeightAwareness.com, http://www.weightawareness.com/topics/doc.xml?doc_id=1374&__topic_id=1114 (accessed June 30, 2005).

5. *Walking: The Natural Way to Fun and Fitness*, produced by the American Heart Association. Also consult the Web sites http://www.americanheart.org and http://walking.about.com/od/healthbenefits/.

6. T. Satoh, et al., "Walking Exercise and Improved Neuropsychological Functioning in Elderly Patients With Cardiac Disease," *Journal of Internal Medicine* 238(5) (1995): 423–428. The conclusion of this study was that the mental activity of elderly cardiac patients with dementia and/or brain atrophy improved with exercise from walking. See also: J. M. Rippe, et al., "Walking for Health and Fitness," *Journal of the American Medical Association* 259(18) (1988): 2720–2724. F. B. Hu, et al., "Walking Compared With Vigorous Physical Activity and Risk of Type 2 Diabetes in Women: A Prospective Study" *Journal of the American Medical Association* 282(15) (1999): 1433–1439. T. F. Jones and C. B. Eaton, "Cost-Benefit Analysis of Walking to Prevent Coronary Heart Disease," *Archives of Family Medicine* 3(8) (1994): 703–710. R. A. Rose, et al., "Effects of Walking on Ventilatory and Cardiac Function in Intact and Cardiac-Impaired Lobsters," *Physiological & Biochemical Zoology* 74(1) (2001): 102–110. (See, exercise is even good for pets, especially pet lobsters.)

7. A Calorie (kcal—1000 calories) is a measure of energy from food; specifically the amount of heat required to raise the temperature of 1 gram of water 1 degree Centigrade.

8. "Activity Calorie Calculator," Fitness Partner Connection Jumpsite!, http://www.primusweb.com/fitnesspartner/jumpsite/calculat.htm (accessed June 30, 2005).

9. "Shorter, More Frequent Exercise Demonstrates Stronger Heart Health Benefits Than One Longer Exercise Session," News Target, http://www.newstarget.com/002462.html, posted November 21, 2004 (accessed June 30, 2005).

10. Bob Anderson, et al., *Getting in Shape* (Bolinas, CA: Shelter Publications, 1994).

11. M. Billiard and A. Bentley, "Is Insomnia Best Categorized as a Symptom or a Disease?" *Sleep Medicine* 5(Suppl 1) (2004): S35–40. A. D. Krystal, "Depression and Insomnia in Women," *Clinical Cornerstone* 6(Suppl 1B) (2004): S19–28. M. Novak, et al., "Increased Utilization of Health Services by Insomniacs—an Epidemiological Perspective." *Journal of Psychosomatic Research* 56(5) (2004): 527–536. D. Foley, et al., "Sleep Disturbances and Chronic Disease in Older Adults: Results of the 2003 National Sleep Foundation Sleep in America Survey," *Journal of Psychosomatic Research* 56(5) (2004): 497–502. C. L. Drake, et al., "Insomnia Causes, Consequences, and Therapeutics: An Overview," *Depression & Anxiety* 18(4) (2003): 163–176. C. H. Schenck, et al., "Assessment and Management of Insomnia," *Journal of the American Medical Association* 289(19) (2003): 2475–2479.

12. Used by permission.

13. We are especially indebted in this section to material from the book *Dr. Mercola's Total Health Cookbook & Program* (Schaumburg, IL: Mercola.com, 2004).

14. REM stands for rapid-eye movement. Before the early 1950s, scientists believed that sleep was primarily dormant, when nothing much was happening in the brain. But in 1953, it was discovered that REM sleep, marked by rapid bursts of eye movements, was a period of sleep during which dreaming occurs. REM sleep has been shown to be an important factor for physical and emotional health.

Chapter 5: Eat and Drink Healthy Things

1. A recent study determined that only 1 percent of youths between the ages of two and nineteen actually consumed the USDA-recommended number of daily servings from all five food groups (grain, vegetable, fruit, dairy, meat), and 16 percent failed to consume the recommended number of servings from *any* food group. See K. A. Munoz, et al., "Food Intakes of U.S. Children and Adolescents Compared With Recommendation," *Pediatrics* 100 (1997): 323–329.

2. S. J. Olshansky, et al., "A Potential Decline in Life Expectancy in the United States in the 20th Century," *New England Journal of Medicine* 352 (2005): 1138–1145.

3. "Global Strategy on Diet, Physical Activity and Health," World Health Organization (WHO), http://www.who.int/dietphysicalactivity/publications/facts/obesity/en/ (accessed July 5, 2005).

4. From the Centers for Disease Control and Prevention: *Overweight* refers to increased body weight in relation to height, when compared to some standard of acceptable or desirable weight. Desirable weight standards are derived by using a mathematical formula known as body mass index (BMI), which represents weight levels associated with the lowest overall risk to health. Desirable BMI levels may vary with age and by using actual heights and weights measured and collected on people who are representative of the U.S. population by the National Center for Health Studies. *Obesity* is defined as an excessively high amount of body fat or adipose tissue in relation to lean body mass. Individuals with a BMI of 25 to 29.9 are considered overweight, while individuals with a BMI of 30 or more are considered obese. See "Overweight and Obesity: Defining Overweight and Obesity," http://www.cdc.gov/nccdphp/dnpa/obesity/defining.htm for more information and access to a simple BMI calculator.

5. "Aim for a Health Weight: Information for Patients and the Public," Obesity Education Initiative, National Heart, Lung and Blood Institute, National Institutes of Health, http://www.nhlbi.nih.gov/health/public/heart/obesity/lose_wt/risk.htm (accessed July 5, 2005).

6. Additives that always contain MSG: hydrolyzed protein, hydrolyzed plant protein, hydrolyzed vegetable protein, hydrolyzed oat flour, plant protein extract, sodium caseinate, calcium caseinate, textured protein, yeast extract, autolyzed yeast. Additives that frequently contain MSG: malt extract, malt stock, various flavorings, spices, various seasonings, bouillon, broths, "natural flavoring."

7. From "Shopper's Guide to Pesticides in Produce," Environmental Working Group, http://www.foodnews.org/walletguide.php (accessed July 5, 2005).

8. "U.S. Surgeon General Releases Advisory on Alcohol Use in Pregnancy," News Release, HHS Press Office, February 21, 2005, http://www.hhs.gov/surgeongeneral/pressreleases/sg02222005.html (accessed July 5, 2005).

9. M. B. Engler, et al., "Flavonoid-Rich Dark Chocolate Improves Endothelial Function and Increases Plasma Epicatechin Concentrations in Healthy Adults," *Journal of the American College of Nutrition* 23 (June 2004): 197–204.

10. Linda Bren, "Losing Weight: Start by Counting Calories," *FDA Consumer Magazine* (January/February 2002), available with updates at http://www.fda.gov/fdac/features/2002/102_fat.html for more information on setting weight-loss goals that are healthy—and achieving them. (Accessed July 5, 2005.)

Chapter 6: Take Charge of Your Health

1. As quoted by Dr. Roy E. Vartabedian on the audiotape Nutripoints, copyright © National Safety Associates, P. O. Box 18603, Memphis, TN 38181.

2. "Chronic Disease Prevention," National Center for Chronic Disease Prevention and Health Promotion, http://www.cdc.gov/nccdphp/ (accessed June 24, 2005).

3. Mayo Clinic Staff, "Secondhand Smoke: Protect Yourself From the Dangers," MayoClinic.com, http://www.mayoclinic.com/invoke.cfm?id=CC00023 (accessed July 5, 2005).

4. Ibid.

5. "Common Toxins: Environmental Tobacco Smoke (ETS) or Secondhand Smoke," Healthy Families, Healthy Environment, http://www.healthyfamiliesnow.org/Article_asp-Record=1053.html (accessed July 5, 2005).

6. Ibid.

7. Ibid.

8. "Out of Harm's Way: Preventing Threats to Child Development," Greater Boston Physicians for Social Responsibility, Fall 2002, http://psr.igc.org/CHeasey.eng. Also, "The Healthy Home," Care2 Make a Difference, http://www.care2.com/channels/lifestyle/home#55 (accessed July 5, 2005).

9. Christine Pittel, "How to Make Your Home Nontoxic," *House Beautiful* online, http://magazines.ivillage.com/housebeautiful/decorate/contest/articles/0,,284678_650679,00.html (accessed July 5, 2005).

10. "Out of Harm's Way: Preventing Threats to Child Development."

11. Ibid.

12. "The Inside Story: A Guide to Indoor Air Quality," U.S. Environmental Protection Agency, Indoor Air—Publications, http://www.epa.gov/iaq/pubs/insidest.html#Intro1 (accessed June 21, 2005).

13. "Healthy Environment, Healthy House," MyMotherLode.com Home Improvement, http://www.mymotherlode.com/Home_Improvement/hi_article_healthy_house.html (accessed July 5, 2005).

14. "Indoor Air Pollution," Healthy Families, Healthy Environment, http://healthyfamiliesnow.org/Article_asp-Record=1080.html (accessed July 5, 2005).

15. "Ten Ways to Improve the Air Your Children Breathe," Care2 Make a Difference, http://www.care2.com/channels/solutions/home/787 (accessed July 5, 2005).

16. Annie Berthold-Bond, with Carlene Gibbons, RN, "Successful Steps to Control Four Airborne Allergens," Care2 Make a Difference, see: http://www.care2.com/channels/solutions/home/371 (accessed July 5, 2005). Also, for information on the health effects of dust mites and how to control them, see: "Dust Mites in the Home," FamilyDoctor.org, http://familydoctor.org/683.xml (accessed June 21, 2005).

17. Pittel, "How to Make Your Home Nontoxic."

18. Berthold-Bond, "Successful Steps to Control Four Airborne Allergens."

19. "An Ounce of Prevention: Keeps the Germs Away," National Center for Infectious Disease, http://www.cdc.gov/ncidod/op/ (accessed July 5, 2005).

20. "Why Noise Hurts Our Health—What You Can Do," Care2 Make a Difference, http://www.care2.com/channels/solutions/home/1606 (accessed July 5, 2005).

21. "Annoying Noises Can Trigger Heart Attacks," http://www.cbsnews.com/stories/2004/09/03.

22. "Why Noise Hurts Our Health—What You Can Do."

23. Roger W. Wicke, PhD, "Effects of Music and Sound on Human Health," *Herbalist Review* 1 (2002).

24. Jackie Craven, "Designing the Healthy Home," About.com—Architecture, http://architecture.about.com/cs/buildyourhouse/a/healthyhome.htm.

25. Periodontitis is a disease of the gums and of the bone that supports the teeth in their sockets. Periodontitis, also called *pyorrhea alveolaris*, is the chief cause of tooth loss after age thirty-five. The most common form of periodontitis results from the buildup of plaque on the teeth and gums. Plaque is a sticky mixture of food particles and bacteria. The bacteria and their waste products irritate the gums and produce gingivitis, an inflammation of the gums. If gingivitis is not treated, the gums become swollen and bleed easily, and in time they may recede from the teeth.

26. Nancy Montgomery, "Dental Anxiety: Taking Charge of Your Inner Wimp," Atrium Health Plan, http://myhealth.atriumhealthplan.com/topic/dentalanxietytips (accessed July 5, 2005).

27. Adapted from David L. Stevens, "How to Talk to Your Doctor," *Today's Christian Doctor*, special HealthWise edition (Spring/Summer 1996): 26–27. Used by permission.

28. "Simple Steps for Taking Charge of Your Personal Health," Pioneer Thinking, http://www.pioneerthinking.com/ara-personalhealth.html (accessed July 5, 2005).

29. Ibid.

30. Ibid.

Chapter 7: Nurture and Protect Your Relationships

1. Elaine Zablocki, "Love's Not Only Good for the Soul," WebMD Medical News, February 14, 2001, http://my.webmd.com/content/Article/30/1728_72337 .htm (accessed June 27, 2005).

2. S. Cohen and T. A. Willis, "Stress, Social Support, and the Buffering Hypothesis," *Psychological Bulletin* 98 (1985): 310–357. L. K. George, "Social Factors and the Onset and Outcome of Depression," in K. W. Schaie, et al., eds., *Aging, Health Behaviors, and Health Outcomes* (Hillsdale, NJ: Lawrence Erlbaum Associates, 1992), 137–159. L. K. George, et al., "Social Support and the Outcome of Major Depression," *British Journal of Psychiatry* 154 (1989): 478–485.

3. L. F. Berkman and S. L. Syme, "Social Networks, Holds Resistance, and Mortality," *American Journal of Epidemiology* 109 (1979): 186–204. T. M. Vogt, et al., "Social Networks as Predictors of Ischemic Heart Disease, Cancer, Stroke and Hypertension," *Journal of Clinical Epidemiology* 45 (1992): 659–666. J. S. House, et al., "Social Relationships and Health," *Science* 241 (1988): 540–545.

4. J. K. Kiecolt-Glaser, et al., "Stressful Personal Relationships: Immune and Into Credit Function," in R. Glaser and J. Kiecolt-Glaser, eds., *Handbook of Human Stress and Immunity* (San Diego, CA: Academic Press, 1994), 321–339. S. Cohen, et al., "Social Ties and Susceptibility to the Common Cold," *Journal of the American Medical Association* 277 (1997): 1940–1944.

5. L. F. Berkman and L. Breslow, *Health and Ways of Living: The Alameda County Study* (New York: Oxford University Press, 1994).

6. C. Dickens, *Heart* 90 (April 2004): 518–522, as referenced in Jeanie Lerche Davis, "Close Relationship Helps Heart," WebMD Medical News, April 14, 2004, http://my.webmd.com/content/Article/85/98683.htm (accessed July 6, 2005).

7. Denise Mann, "Friendship: Good for What Ails You," WebMD Medical News, March 21, 2001, http://my.webmd.com/content/article/31/1728_75265.htm (accessed July 6, 2005).

8. "Together We Do Better Health Facts," VicHealth, http://www .togetherwedobetter.vic.gov.au/healthfacts/ (accessed July 6, 2005). See also L. Syme, "Rethinking Disease: Where Do We Go From Here?" *AEP* 6.5 (1996): 463–468.

9. "Health Benefits of Marriage," The Care Center, http://teencarecenter.com/ index.php?s=factsheets&p=sheet15.

10. Maggie Gallagher, "Why Marriage Is Good for You," *City Journal*, Autumn 2000, http://www.city-journal.org/html/10_4_why_marriage_is.html (accessed June 20, 2005).

11. "Sex, Marriage, and Family—the Lutheran Church in America: A Social Statement of the Lutheran Church in America, adopted by the Fifth Biennial Convention," Minneapolis, MN, June 25–July 2, 1970.

12. The ideas in this section are adapted from material at "Building Family Strengths—Unity," Clemson University Cooperative Extension Service: Family Relationships, January 1998, http://virtual.clemson.edu/groups/psapublishing/ Pages/FYD/FL522.pdf (accessed June 27, 2005).

13. The ideas in this section are adapted from material at "Strengthening Family Relationships," Advocates for Youth, http://www.advocatesforyouth.org/publications/pccbasics/packet/strengthen.htm (accessed June 27, 2005).

14. Jennifer Warner, "Supportive Parents Promote Good Health," WebMD Medical News, March 24, 2004, http://aolsvc.health.webmd.aol.com/content/Article/84/98135.htm (accessed June 27, 2005).

15. Ideas in this section are adapted from Lori Palatnik, "Honoring Parents," http://www.aish.com/literacy/mitzvahs/Honoring_Parents.asp (accessed July 6, 2005), from her book *Remember My Soul*, as well as other sources.

16. T. E. Oxman, et al., "Social Support and Depressive Symptoms in the Elderly," *American Journal of Epidemiology* 135(4) (1992): 356–368. R. H. Moos, "Depressed Outpatients' Life Contexts, Amount of Treatment, and Treatment Outcome," *Journal of Nervous & Mental Disease* 178(2) (1990): 105–112.

17. R. B. Williams, et al., "Prognostic Importance of Social and Economic Resources Among Medically Treated Patients With Angiographically Documented Coronary Artery Disease," *Journal of the American Medical Association* 267(4) (1992): 520–524.

18. Some material in this section is adapted from "True Friendship—Trust & Time," http://www.allaboutgod.com/true-friendship.htm (accessed July 6, 2005).

19. For extraordinary insights into this process, see Lewis B. Smedes, *Forgive and Forget* (New York: HarperCollins, 1984).

20. Mary Duenwald, "The Benefits of Forgiveness," LHJ.com, http://www.lhj.com/lhj/story.jhtml?storyid=/templatedata/lhj/story/data/HealthNews_Forgiveness_05052003.xml (accessed June 27, 2005).

21. "People Who Forgive Feel Better," PreventDisease.com, http://www.preventdisease.com/lifestyle/emotion/articles/people_who_forgive_feel_better.html (accessed July 6, 2005).

22. If you don't know the story, see John 13:38; Luke 22:54–61; John 21:4–17.

Chapter 8: Don't Worry, Be Happy

1. Claudia Wallis, "The New Science of Happiness," *Time*, January 17, 2005.

2. According to Seligman: "The term *happiness* itself is too slippery to be of much use scientifically. However, it can be usefully broken down into three domains, each of which can be reliably measured, and what's more, each of which you can build into your own life...." See: http://reflectivehappiness.com/abouthappiness.htm (accessed July 6, 2005).

3. University of Wisconsin, *HealthEmotions Research Institute University of Wisconsin*, "Current Projects of the HealthEmotions Research Institute," http://www.healthemotions.org (accessed July 19, 2005).

4. Dr. David Demko, *AgeVenture*, "If You Don't Long to Live, You Won't Live Too Long," http://www.demko.com/m990705.htm (accessed July 19, 2005). See also: D. D. Danner, et al., "Positive Emotions in Early Life and Longevity: Findings From the Nun Study," *Journal of Personality and Social Psychology* 80 (May 2001): 804. See also: B. Rabin, *Stress, Immune Function and Health* (New

York: Wiley-Liss, 1999), which supports the fact that happiness is associated with lower stress levels, a definite health benefit, since over time, stress can affect the cardiovascular system, the immune system, and the endocrine system adversely.

5. Rich Bayer, PhD, "The Benefits of Happiness," Upper Bay Counseling and Support Services, Inc., http://www.upperbay.org/benefits_of_happiness.html (accessed July 19, 2005).

6. Michael D. Lemonick, "The Biology of Joy," *Time*, January 17, 2005.

7. Ibid.

8. Frederic Flach, *Resilience* (New York: Random House, 1988), xiii–xiv.

9. Ibid., 259.

10. David Niven, PhD, *The 100 Simple Secrets of Happy People* (New York: HarperCollins, 2000), 41–42. "A study of life satisfaction looked at twenty different factors that might contribute to happiness. Nineteen of those factors did matter, and one did not. The one factor that did not matter was financial status." (Ibid., 190).

11. The Gallup Organization, "Gallup Study: Unhappy Workers Are Unhealthy Too," Gallup Management Journal, http://gmj.gallup.com/print/?ci=14545, (accessed July 19, 2005). Also: Datadome, "70% Employee Disengagement?," WorkForce Trends Newsletter August 2004, Volume 3, Issue 3, 2004, http://www.datadome.com/worktrends3_3.html (accessed July 19, 2005).

12. Brother Lawrence, *The Practice of the Presence of God* (New Kensington, PA: Whitaker House, 1992).

13. Donald W. McCullough, *Finding Happiness in the Most Unlikely Places* (Downer's Grove, IL: InterVarsity Press, 1990), 158–159.

14. One of the findings of the now famous, and ongoing, "Nun Study," is that those who expressed positive emotions early in life in their journals ended up outliving others whose journal entries were not so positive. See: David Snowdon, *Aging with Grace* (New York: Bantam, 2001). See also: Robert A. Emmons and Joanna Hill, *Words of Gratitude for Mind, Body, and Soul* (Templeton Press), in which they claim that "not only are those who practice gratitude happier, they are also healthier, exercise more frequently, and are more apt to be helpful to others."

15. See multiple scriptures, including: Psalm 106:1; 107:1; 118:1; 136:1; Romans 1:21 (related to those who reject God by not giving Him thanks and what happens as a result); Ephesians 5:20; Colossians 1:12; 3:17; and 1 Thessalonians 5:18.

16. In 1990, Judith Siegel from the University of California, Los Angeles, reported in the *Journal of Personality and Social Psychology* that elderly people who owned a pet needed fewer doctor visits. Her examination of almost 1,000 Medicare recipients took into account a person's living conditions, underlying chronic disease, education, and other factors known to influence health. She found that people without pets average 9.49 visits to the doctor in one year, while pet owners had only 8.42 visits during the year studied.

17. Dr. Joseph Mercola with Laina Krisik, "Man's Best Friend Adds Years of Happiness to Your Life," http://www.mercola.com/fcgi/pf/2004/nov/17/dogs_health.htm (accessed July 19, 2005).

Chapter 9: Help Somebody Else

1. Hans Selye, *The Stress of Life* (New York: McGraw-Hill, 1956).

2. Allan Luks, "Helper's High: Volunteering Makes People Feel Good, Physically and Emotionally. And Like 'Runner's Calm,' It's Probably Good for Your Health," *Psychology Today* (1988): 39, 42.

3. The Random Acts of Kindness Foundation, "Kindness: How Good Deeds Can Be Good for You!" Inspiration: Health Benefits, http://www.actsofkindness .org/inspiration/health/detail.asp?id=1 (accessed July 19, 2005).

4. Allan Luks and Peggy Payne, *The Healing Power of Doing Good: The Health and Spiritual Benefits of Helping Others* (New York: iUniverse, 2001).

5. For more information, visit these Web sites: http://helpothers.org/pif/ or http://www.actsofkindness.org/.

6. The Random Acts of Kindness Foundation, "Health Benefits of Kindness— Abbreviated."

7. Ken Wilson and Virgil Gulker, *Helping You Is Helping Me* (Ann Arbor, MI: Servant Publications, 1993), 29–38.

8. Linda P. Fried, et al., 2004, "A Social Model for Health Promotion for an Aging Population: Initial Evidence on the Experience Corps Model," Abstract, *Journal of Urban Health* 81(1) (2004): 64–78.

9. D. C. McClelland and C. Kirshnit, "The Effect of Motivational Arousal Through Films on Salivary Immunoglobulin A," *Journal of Psychology and Health* 2 (1988): 31–52.

10. Paul Brand and Philip Yancey, *In His Image* (Grand Rapids: Zondervan, 1984), 43–46.

Chapter 10: Discover Your Purpose

1. Marianna Krejci-Papa, "Better in the Long Run," *Science and Spirit*, March 23, 2002, http://www.science-spirit.org/printerfriendly.php?article_id=483 (accessed July 20, 2005).

2. Daniel DeNoon, reviewed by Brunilda Nazario, MD, "Immune System Boosted in Those Who Find Meaning in Grief," April 30, 2003, WebMD Medical News, http://my.webmd.com/content/Article/64/72308.htm?printing=true (accessed July 20, 2005).

3. News-Medical.Net, August 15, 2004, "Good Health Goes Beyond Diet, Exercise and Stress," Medical Research News, http://www.news-medical.net/print_ article.asp?id=4074 (accessed July 20, 2005).

4. Ibid.

5. David Niven, PhD, *The 100 Simple Secrets of Happy People* (New York: HarperCollins, 2000), 1.

6. Stephen R. Covey, *The 7 Habits of Highly Effective People* (New York: Simon & Schuster, 1989), 98.

Chapter 11: Practice Your Faith

1. H. G. Koenig, et al., "The Relationship Between Religious Activities and Blood Pressure in Older Adults," *International Journal of Psychiatry in Medicine* 28(2) (1998): 189–213.

2. U. Goldbourt, et al., 1993, "Factors Predictive of Long-Term Coronary Heart Disease Mortality Among 10,059 Male Israeli Civil Servants and Municipal Employees," *Cardiology* 82 (1993): 100–121.

3. P. H. Van Ness, et al., "Religion, Race, and Breast Cancer Survival," *International Journal of Psychiatry in Medicine* 33 (2003): 357–376.

4. J. E. Enstrom, "Health Practices and Cancer Mortality Among Active California Mormons," *Journal of the National Cancer Institute* 31 (1989): 1807–1814.

5. H. G. Koenig, et al., "Attendance at Religious Services, Interleukin-6, and Other Biological Parameters of Immune Function in Older Adults," *International Journal of Psychiatry in Medicine* 27(3) (1997): 233–250.

6. S. K. Lutgendorf, et al., "Religious Participation, Interleukin-6, and Mortality in Older Adults," *Health Psychology*, 23(5) (2004): 465–475.

7. S. E. Sephton, et al., "Spiritual Expression and Immune Status in Women With Metastatic Breast Cancer: An Exploratory Study," *Breast Journal* 7(5) (2001): 345–353.

8. G. Ironson, et al., "The Ironson-Woods Spirituality/Religiousness Index Is Associated With Long Survival, Health Behaviors, Less Distress, and Low Cortisol in People With HIV/AIDS," *Annals of Behavioral Medicine* 24(1) (Winter 2002): 34–48.

9. T. E. Woods, et al., "Religiosity Is Associated With Affective and Immune Status in Symptomatic HIV-Infected Gay Men," *Journal of Psychosomatic Research* 46 (1999): 165–176.

10. E. A. Dedert, et al., "Private Religious Practice: Protection of Cortisol Rhythms Among Women With Fibromyalgia," *International Journal of Psychiatry in Medicine* 34 (2004): 61–77.

11. T. E. Oxman, et al., "Lack of Social Participation or Religious Strength and Comfort as Risk Factors for Death After Cardiac Surgery in the Elderly," *Psychosomatic Medicine* 57 (1995): 5–15.

12. R. J. Contrada, et al., "Psychosocial Factors in Outcomes of Heart Surgery: The Impact of Religious Involvement and Depressive Symptoms," *Health Psychology* 23 (2004): 227–238.

13. H. G. Koenig and D. B. Larson, "Use of Hospital Services, Church Attendance, and Religious Affiliation," *Southern Medical Journal* 91 (1998): 925–932.

14. H. G. Koenig, et al., "Religion, Spirituality, Acute Hospital and Long-Term Care Use by Older Patients," *Archives of Internal Medicine* 164 (2004): 1579–1585.

15. H. M. Helm, et al., "Does Private Religious Activity Prolong Survival? A Six-Year Follow-up Study of 3,851 Older Adults," *Journals of Gerontology Series A—Biological Sciences and Medical Sciences* 55(7) (July 2000): M400–405.

16. H. G. Koenig, et al., "Does Religious Attendance Prolong Survival? A Six-Year Follow-up Study of 3,968 Older Adults," *Journals of Gerontology Series A—Biological Sciences and Medical Sciences* 54(7) (1999): M370–376.

17. W. J. Strawbridge, et al., "Frequent Attendance at Religious Services and Mortality Over 28 Years," *American Journal of Public Health* 87(6) (June 1997): 957–961.

18. R. Hummer, et al., "Religious Involvement and U.S. Adult Mortality," *Demography* 36 (1999): 273–285.

19. M. H. Monroe, et al., "Primary Care Physician Preferences Regarding Spiritual Behavior in Medical Practice," *Archives of Internal Medicine* 163(22) (2003): 2751–2756. See also: D. E. King, et al., "Experiences and Attitudes About Faith Healing Among Family Physicians," *Journal of Family Practice* 35(2) (1992): 158–162.

20. Ibid.

21. J. T. Chibnall and C. A. Brooks, "Religion in the Clinic: The Role of Physician Beliefs," *Southern Medical Journal* 94 (2001): 374–379. Also, D. E. King and B. J. Wells, "End-of-Life Issues and Spiritual Histories," *Southern Medical Journal* 96(4) (2003): 391–393.

22. P. A. Clark, et al., "Addressing Patients' Emotional and Spiritual Needs," *Joint Commission Journal on Quality and Safety* 29 (2003): 659–670.

23. To order this book, or for information about the ministries of CMDA or to access a list of specific members practicing in your area, visit www.cmdahome. org or write: CMDA, P. O. Box 7500, Bristol, TN 37621, or call: (423) 844-1000.

24. H. Carter and P. C. Glick, "Marriage and Divorce: A Social and Economic Study, American Public Health Association," *Vital and Health Statistics Monograph* (Cambridge: Harvard University Press, 1970). Also, J. J. Lynch, *The Broken Heart: The Medical Consequences of Loneliness* (New York, NY: Basic Books, 1977), quoted in "Fact Sheet: Divorce and Health," Rocky Mountain Family Council, http://www.rmfc.org/fs/fs0054.html (accessed July 21, 2005).

25. For more information on the benefits of support groups visit these Web sites: http://community.healthgate.com, http://www.supportfind.com, http://www .sleepquest.com, http://www.lifeway.com, http://www.womenshealthmatters.com, http://www.psychosocial.com.

26. K. I. Pargament, et al., "Religious Struggle as a Predictor of Mortality Among Medically Ill Elderly Patients: A Two-Year Longitudinal Study," *Archives of Internal Medicine* 161 (2001): 1881–1885.

Additional Resources Related to Health and Faith

By Harold G. Koenig, MD

Is Religion Good for Your Health? (Haworth Press, 1997)

Healing Power of Faith (Simon & Schuster, 1999)

Handbook of Religion and Health (Oxford University Press, 2001)

Spirituality in Patient Care (Templeton Press, 2002)

Faith and Mental Health: Religious Resources for Healing (Templeton Press, 2005)

By David B. Biebel, DMin

Jonathan, You Left Too Soon (Spire, 1997—available only from the author; see Biosketch for contact information)

If God Is So Good, Why Do I Hurt So Bad? (Baker, 2005 reprint)

How to Help a Heartbroken Friend (Hope Publishing House, rev 2004)

New Light on Depression (Zondervan, 2004), Gold Medallion winner, with Harold G. Koenig, MD

Other books

The Faith Factor by Dale Matthews, MD (Viking)

The Psychology of Religion and Coping by Ken Pargament, PhD (Guilford Press)

The "Highly Healthy" series by Walt Larimore, MD (Zondervan)

Margin and *The Overload Syndrome* by Richard Swenson, MD (NavPress)

My Big Fat Greek Diet by Nick Yphantides, MD (Nelson)

SIMPLE HEALTH

Internet resources

Various quizzes and lists from this book, research updates, and health-related information augmenting *Simple Health* can be found on Dave Biebel's Web site: www.crosshearthealth.com.

Other health-related Web sites

www.mercola.com
www.webmd.com
www.siloam.com
www.christianwellness.org
www.cmda.org
www.dukespiritualityandhealth.org
www.nihr.org

Biosketch

Harold G. Koenig, MD, MHSc is board certified in general psychiatry, geriatric psychiatry, and geriatric medicine. He is on the faculty at Duke University as professor of psychiatry and behavioral sciences and associate professor of medicine. Dr. Koenig is codirector of the Center for Spirituality, Theology and Health at Duke University Medical Center, and has published extensively in the fields of mental health, geriatrics, and religion, with more than 250 scientific peer-reviewed articles and book chapters and 29 books in print or in preparation. He is editor of the *International Journal of Psychiatry in Medicine* and is founder and editor-in-chief of *Science and Theology News*. His research on religion, health, and ethical issues in medicine has been featured on more than 50 national and international TV news programs (including recently *The Today Show* and two episodes of *Good Morning America*), 80 national or international radio programs, and hundreds of newspapers and magazines (including cover stories for *Reader's Digest, Parade, Newsweek,* and *Time*). Dr. Koenig has given testimony before the U.S. Senate concerning the benefits of religion and spirituality on health. Dr. Koenig has also given hundreds of seminars and workshops (see www.dukespiritualityandhealth.org). To arrange a speaking engagement, contact Dr. Koenig by e-mail at koenig@geri.duke.edu.

David B. Biebel, DMin, holds a doctor of ministry degree in personal wholeness from Gordon-Conwell Theological Seminary. He has authored or coauthored more than a dozen books, including the bestseller *If God Is So Good, Why Do I Hurt So Bad?*, its companion volume *How to Help a Heartbroken Friend, Finding Your Way After the Suicide of Someone You Love* (2005), and the Gold Medallion–winning *New Light on Depression* (2004), which he did with Dr.Koenig. He has edited *Today's Christian Doctor* for the Christian Medical & Dental Associations since 1992. He is an expert on recovery from losses; a speaker at workshops, seminars, and retreats; and a frequent radio and TV guest. He cofounded Hope Central Ministries (www .hopecentral.us) to minister God's healing grace to those who hurt. He and his wife, Ilona, are health educators in person and via their Web site: www.crosshearthealth.com. They live in Colorado, where they enjoy bowhunting for elk and deer, mushrooming, fishing, camping, and otherwise roaming the beautiful Rockies. Dr. Biebel fancies himself a gourmet cook and sometimes refers to himself in the third person, especially when his burnt offerings are suitable only for his English Springer spaniel, Brownie. He may be reached by e-mail at dbbv1@aol.com.

Strang Communications, the publisher of both Charisma House and *Charisma* magazine, wants to give you 3 FREE ISSUES of our award-winning magazine.

Since its inception in 1975, *Charisma* magazine has helped thousands of Christians stay connected with what God is doing worldwide.

Within its pages you will discover in-depth reports and the latest news from a Christian perspective, biblical health tips, global events in the body of Christ, personality profiles, and so much more. Join the family of *Charisma* readers who enjoy feeding their spirit each month with miracle-filled testimonies and inspiring articles that bring clarity, provoke prayer, and demand answers.

To claim your **3 free issues** of *Charisma,* send your name and address to: Charisma 3 Free Issue Offer, 600 Rinehart Road, Lake Mary, FL 32746. Or you may call 1-800-829-3346 and ask for Offer # 93FREE. This offer is only valid in the USA.

---

www.charismamag.com

3581